The
Green Witch's Guide to
Magical Plants
&
Flowers

—◦⟩⟨◦—

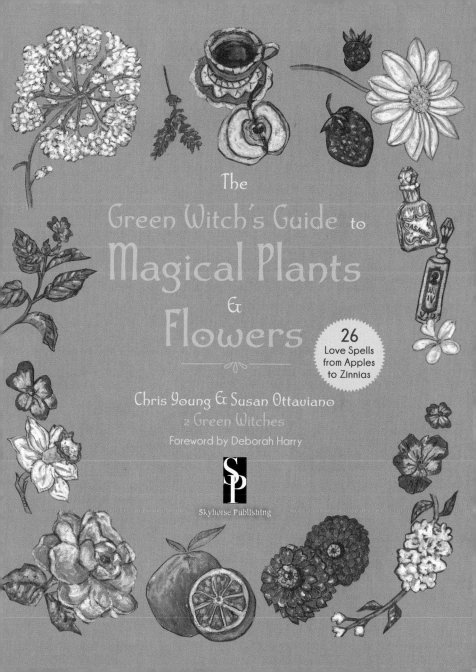

The
Green Witch's Guide to
Magical Plants
&
Flowers

26 Love Spells from Apples to Zinnias

Chris Young & Susan Ottaviano
2 Green Witches

Foreword by Deborah Harry

Skyhorse Publishing

Skyhorse Publishing books may be purchased in bulk at special discounts
for sales promotion, corporate gifts, fund-raising, or educational purposes.
Special editions can also be created to specifications. For details, contact
the Special Sales Department, Skyhorse Publishing, 307 West 36th Street,
11th Floor, New York, NY 10018 or info@skyhorsepublishing.com.

Skyhorse® and Skyhorse Publishing® are registered trademarks of Skyhorse
Publishing, Inc.®, a Delaware corporation.

Visit our website at www.skyhorsepublishing.com.

10 9 8 7 6 5 4 3 2

Library of Congress Cataloging-in-Publication Data is available on file.

Cover design by David Ter Avanesyan
Cover illustrations by Susan Ottaviano

Print ISBN: 978-1-5107-7566-4
Ebook ISBN: 978-1-5107-7567-1

Printed in China

THIS BOOK BELONGS TO

❧ TABLE OF CONTENTS ❧

❧ FOREWORD ☙

I was invited to visit Chris Young's home while I was in LA.
Having known him for years when he was a younger Blondie fan,
and having some downtime in between shows, I said yes to this
invitation. LA, like many cities with a history, has a lot of hidden
curiosities, a wealth of places tucked away in the hills or at the
dead end of a street that appears to trail off into the Pacific. When I
arrived at Chris's place, he showed me around his charming house,
then said let's go outside into the garden. This is where I learned
something about him that I never knew: Chris has a passion for
creating habitats of beauty with all the sweet, spicy, earthy smells
that come along with the flowers, trees, paths, and ponds. I could
even smell the sunshine. Immediately, I was transported to another
dimension. What an incredible surprise it was finding out another
side of Chris's personality! Now, years later, Chris and his friend
Susan Ottaviano have put together *The Green Witch's Guide to
Magical Plants & Flowers: Love Spells from Apples to Zinnias.* I
can think of more than a few friends who would love to have this
book, which is full of info, recipes, illustrations, and lots of stories,
history, and lore. As for myself, I think this book is a keeper, and I
will have it on my shelf within easy reach for the next time I want to
cast a love spell on the object of my affection. I love surprises, and
this collection is a really good one!

—Deborah Harry

Imagine yourself calmly strolling through a beautiful flower-filled garden with the gentle sounds of birds singing, and bees and butterflies dancing from flower to flower. Perhaps there is an old apple tree heavy with ruby red apples. There are herbs such as basil, parsley, and rosemary growing along the path, and the scent of lavender and jasmine fill the air. You can't help but breathe in all the sweet smells. A small pond is home to water lilies and little fish, with fairy-like dragonflies darting about. The garden is so peaceful. You might say it's enchanted. And it is! Let it enchant you. Slow down. Stop and smell the roses, literally. What if you not only smell the roses, but you also touch and really observe them? While you're there, what if you become very still and listen to all the sounds around you? You would be experiencing "magical mindfulness." Let Chris and Susan, your two new green witch friends, teach you to use elements you find there to make magical spells and harness the power that lies within your garden!

Susan and I have been friends for over thirty years. Our common interests in nature and mindfulness have naturally drawn us into the mystical world of green witchcraft. As a young adult going through a really difficult time in my life, I was lucky enough to meet a green witch named Irma. She taught me simple little spells to calm and ground myself by using what Susan and I like to call magical mindfulness. With Irma, I learned to make a wreath of birch branches to hang on my door to protect my home from negative energy. She showed me how to cleanse my personal space by using sages and burning onion skins in a small iron cauldron. Irma used magical herbalism to help me heal—and it worked.

The very act of creating the love spells and witch-crafty projects in this book should help you heal as well. Remember always to pause and take a deep breath before a spell and set your intention. If you don't have someone in mind to make the recipes for, simply enjoy them yourself. What could be more soothing than a candlelit bath after a stressful day? We've got that in here for you, along with twenty-six carefully chosen magical herbs and their accompanying soul-soothing spells. Another thing we're really excited about is that all recipes in this book are cruelty-free and 100 percent vegan!

Our shared belief that we could all use more love in our lives, a (re)connection to nature, and a chance to relax inspired us to create this book of spells, or *grimoire,* to help bring more contentment into your life. Now, go out there, turn off your cell phone, breathe deeply, and get your green witch on.

So mote it be!

—Chris

❧ WHAT IS GREEN WITCHCRAFT? ❧

To create and practice green witchcraft, one must embrace a true love of nature. A green witch's connection to earth and the universe allows them to draw great power for creating love, health, peace, blessings, and harmony in their world. They must work their magic using the energy of the sun, moon, and earth via such items as plants and gemstones. All elements from nature can and do possess enchantment. A green witch knows that the most important thing when doing magic is intention. With the best intention, all good magic is possible! The craft is a very personal one to the green witch, who is encouraged to rely upon their own instincts and creativity in making their unique spells. They are not part of a coven. Rather, they are independent and work their magic alone.

Magical herbalism is central to the practice of green witchcraft, and we are adding magical mindfulness for self-care. A green witch ideally grows and nurtures their own plants and flowers in order to better understand the plant's characteristics and uses. They set their intention for the plant to be magical and lovely with every action they take from planting, nurturing, and harvesting. The very act of gardening is a moving meditation.

Always remember: The magic of the green witch is only to be used for good and positivity. A green witch is a champion for the environment and lives their life in a manner that causes the least damage to beloved Mother Earth. Green witches are also known as hedge witches, garden witches, and kitchen witches. Being a green witch is not specific to any gender—all are welcome!

Keep these items at hand for crafting the recipes and rituals described in this book.

- **Spoons**: Various shapes and sizes, including a wooden spoon and silicone spatula for using with nonstick pans
- **Mixing bowls**: Assorted sizes
- **Mortar and pestle**: Some of the herbs and ingredients will need to be ground or blended
- **Double boiler**: Makes candles and soap, and tempers chocolate. A medium saucepan with a metal pan fitted snugly inside can be substituted
- **Glass measuring cup**: For soaps and candles
- **Saucepans**: Small and medium-sized
- **Large skillet/pan**
- **Baking pans**
- **Cauldron or stock pot**
- **Fine mesh strainers**
- **Colander**

- **Stainless steel tongs**
- **Eyedropper**: For adding small quantities to your magical potions
- **Tweezers**: Helpful for working with candles, Candied Violet Flowers (page 199), and more
- **Knives**: Including a chef's knife and a serrated knife
- **Kitchen scissors**: For snipping herbs
- **Parchment paper**: For lining pans
- **Bamboo skewers**: For candle making
- **Spice grinder**
- **Bowls**: Small ceramic and wooden bowls for spices and herbs
- **Jars**: With lids (we like to reuse old pickle or jelly jars); you can never have too many!

❧ TEA ESSENTIALS ❧

- **Teapot**: These are fun to collect and display
- **Tea kettle**: For heating water
- **Tea infuser**: For loose teas
- **Fine mesh tea or cocktail strainer**: To strain herbs from liquids
- **Teacups**: Get creative and collect various styles of teacups and saucers. There are many beautiful vintage, modern, and handmade options to choose from!

BAKING ESSENTIALS

- **Electric hand mixer**
- **Mixing bowls**
- **Two (9-inch) cake pans**
- **Offset spatula:** For icing cakes

- **Food processor**
- **Cupcake trays**
- **Sheet pans**
- **Decorative platter or cake stand** (optional)

GARDENING ESSENTIALS

- **Shovel**
- **Sun hat**
- **Gardening gloves**
- **Clay pots:** Various sizes
- **Orchid pots**
- **Trowel**
- **Garden shears**
- **Rose clippers**

Don't Forget!

Broom: Everyone has a broom, but a witch will have a special one made of natural fibers or herbs created by hand. Brooms are symbols of good luck and for metaphysically sweeping misfortune away. *Never* use this broom for actual housecleaning!

A witch's broom is a protective and purifying tool. Use this broom only to clear your sacred space before a ritual. You may also protect your home by placing it over your front door.

10 WAYS TO BEGIN YOUR ⤳ MAGICAL JOURNEY ⤶

1. Dream. Keep this lovely grimoire next to your bed. Before you drift off to sleep, find a flower within its pages that speaks to you in some way—intuition plays a huge part in being a green witch. Maybe you're drawn to the color or the name or maybe the flower was a favorite of your grandmother's. Imagine what kind of spell you'll do with the flower, just before you close your eyes.

2. Create rituals. Pick out a spell that involves ingredients. Assemble them and lay them out in a way that appeals to you. Choose some flowers to place on your altar. Light some incense. Clean your work area using natural items such as sage, mint, and lemon oil. Do this every time you create magic, and you may find this to be a soothing form of magical mindfulness. We encourage you to focus on self-love and perform this ritual for your own enjoyment and benefit.

3. Meditate. Spend time with a plant that you are drawn to. Touch it and hold it and spend quiet time contemplating its beauty and powers. Notice how relaxing, calming, and grounding this can be.

4. Explore. If it's not a plant that is already growing in your garden or flower box, take a field trip to a local botanical garden or nursery to see the plant growing naturally. You'll find that walking around a botanical garden or nursery is time well spent!

5. Set your intentions. As you perform your spell, try to stay focused on the outcome as well as the simple pleasure of creating it. Every step of the way can and should be a form of magical mindfulness. Remember that these love spells do not have to be performed for anyone in particular.

6. Make time for yourself. When preparing a magical bath with rose or jasmine, light some candles and put on some soothing music. Enjoy your time recharging in the luxurious soak you have created.

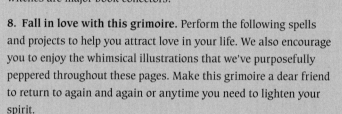

7. Research. Find some books about plants and read about where the flowers you will be working with are from. Imagine what the culture and geography is like where they occur naturally. The Internet will also provide loads of photos and information on the plant you will be working with. It's always more fun to visit a bookstore or library, though. Many of us green witches are major book collectors!

8. Fall in love with this grimoire. Perform the following spells and projects to help you attract love in your life. We also encourage you to enjoy the whimsical illustrations that we've purposefully peppered throughout these pages. Make this grimoire a dear friend to return to again and again or anytime you need to lighten your spirit.

9. Ground yourself. The very act of creating these love spells will serve as a way for you to be present in each moment and take your mind away from the daily stresses of life. Enjoy the work. Green witchcraft is magical mindfulness at its best.

10. Get witchy! You may have never practiced any form of witchcraft up until now, so this is the time to really go for it. Look in the mirror while holding your book to your heart and say, "I am a green witch. So mote it be!" Now, go and make some beautiful magic!

APPLE

(THE TREE OF LOVE)

(Malus pumila)

The humble apple is an ancient symbol of immortality. It is a beautiful, medium-sized deciduous tree covered in white to pink blooms in spring and lovely round golden to red fruit in summer and autumn. It has been in cultivation for thousands of years, not just because it's a delicious food, but also due to the fact that its magical properties include love, fertility, protection, and longevity. Medicinally, apples are said to help lower the risk of heart disease and regular consumption is reported to help with memory loss. Apples are perfect in love spells, as the tree is in the sign of Aphrodite—the ancient Greek goddess of love, desire, sex, and beauty. An added bonus is that apples are delicious, so most love spells naturally involve eating them!

2 GREEN WITCHES SAYETH

"To create a love spell
that is simple and true,
have your crush share
an apple with you."

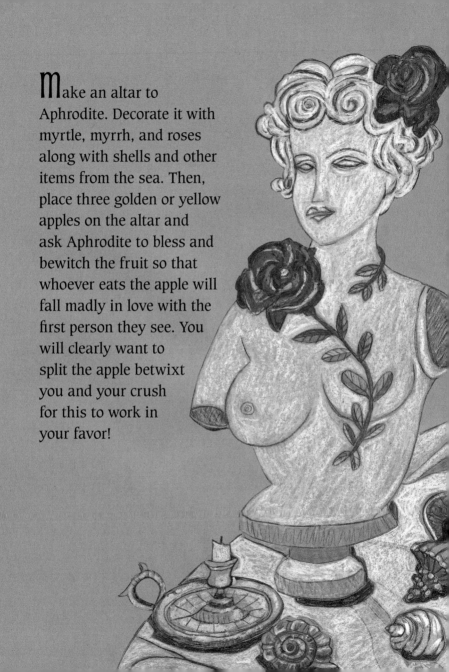

Make an altar to Aphrodite. Decorate it with myrtle, myrrh, and roses along with shells and other items from the sea. Then, place three golden or yellow apples on the altar and ask Aphrodite to bless and bewitch the fruit so that whoever eats the apple will fall madly in love with the first person they see. You will clearly want to split the apple betwixt you and your crush for this to work in your favor!

ANCIENT GREEK APPLE LOVE SPELL

∞ Magical ∞
Mindfulness Tip

This is a wonderfully relaxing tea to savor
alone. The enchanting scents of clove
and cinnamon offer protection and aid in
meditation and healing.

APPLE LOVER'S TEA

(SERVES 2)

Since ancient times, sharing an apple with the apple of your eye has been an enchanting way to gain their interest. We suggest you try making this magical tea for two!

2 green tea bags
2 sticks cinnamon
3 cloves
4 whole allspice berries
1 cup unsweetened organic apple
  juice or apple cider

1 green organic apple, sliced
Organic maple syrup or organic
  sugar, to taste

In a saucepan, bring 2 cups of water to a boil. Add tea bags, cinnamon, cloves, and allspice to the pan. Remove from the heat; cover and let steep for 3 minutes. Discard tea bags and spices into your compost bin. Stir in apple juice or cider and heat through.

(Always remember that spoons are a kind of wand. You can use them while you cook to direct your energy and intentions to empower whatever you are preparing!)

Pour into teacups.

Serve with green apple slices and maple syrup or sugar, to taste.

MAGICAL PROPERTIES OF APPLE LOVER'S TEA

Green tea (Camellia) = riches

Allspice = luck

Apples = love

Cinnamon = protection

Cloves = love and protection

Sugar = healing and sweetness

Maple (syrup) = love and healing

APPLE BINDING SPELL

Carve a big red apple as you might a pumpkin for All Hallows' Eve—only carve a heart on the front in lieu of a scary jack-o'-lantern face! As with a pumpkin, cut the top off the apple so that it may act as a lid. Core out the center of the apple and replace the seeds with a small piece of paper with the name of your crush written on it. Also include your photo and bind them with a dollop of maple syrup, then close your apple and bury it. To strengthen the spell, bury the carved apple under a young apple tree during a full moon.

GREEN THUMB

Plant bare-root trees in winter or early spring ideally under a full moon in fertile, compost-rich, well-drained soil. Water regularly. Be especially vigilant that the soil doesn't dry out through the first summer.

Apple trees can reach twenty feet tall
and begin bearing fruit
within six to ten years.

To honor Aphrodite,
place a ring of seashells
around the base
of your young tree.

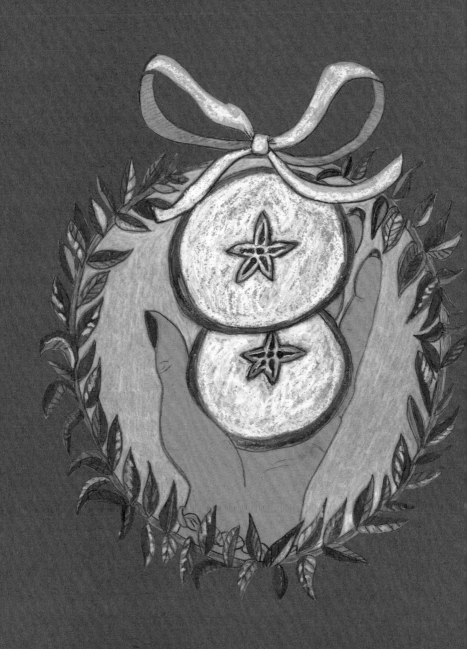

DID YOU KNOW?

Have you ever noticed that when an apple is sliced laterally, the seeds form a five-pointed star, the mystical and magical symbol of the pentagram? To witches, the apple tree is pure magic, as pentagrams are associated with protection and luck. Stargazers even use the five position points to track the morning star in the heavens over an eight-year period.

2 GREEN WITCHES SAYETH

"Basil, basil, fresh and sweet,
allow two angry hearts to meet."

(THE WITCH'S HERB)
(Ocimum basilicum)

Basil is an ancient healing herb that has been used for ages in Ayurvedic medicine. Basil is in the mint family and, like all mints, is very aromatic and beloved by pollinators. Cooking basil is often done with the annual common version, which has pretty pointed leaves and lovely tiny cones of flowers. It is known magically to bring luck and harmony.

STRESS RELIEF SPELL IN LOVE

Wear a lace sachet filled with fresh shredded or dried basil leaves around your neck or lay fresh basil over black charcoal burning in a deep bowl or small cauldron. This simple spell should relieve any stress you are feeling in your relationship.

BASIL LOVER'S PESTO

(MAKES 1 CUP)

½ cup pine nuts or walnuts
4 cups packed fresh basil leaves
2 large garlic cloves, minced
⅓ cup extra virgin olive oil
Salt and pepper, to taste

Preheat the oven to 375°F. Place nuts on a medium-sized baking pan. Toast the nuts until golden brown, about 5 to 10 minutes. Watch carefully, as the nuts can burn.

Add all ingredients to a food processor and process until smooth. Season with salt and pepper, to taste.

Pesto may be made two days ahead of time. Store in the fridge covered with plastic wrap.

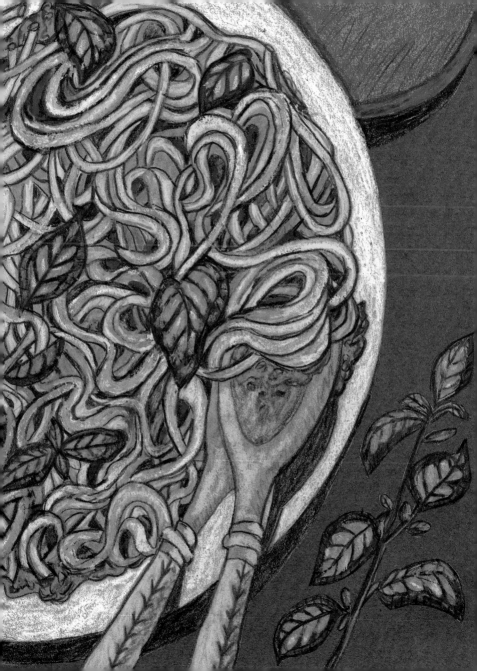

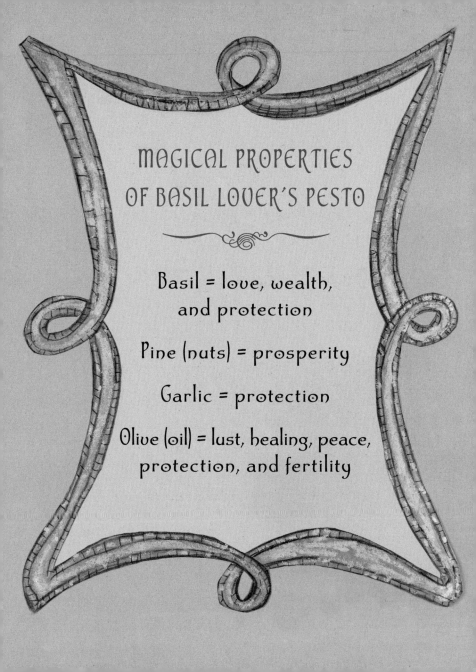

MAGICAL PROPERTIES OF BASIL LOVER'S PESTO

Basil = love, wealth, and protection

Pine (nuts) = prosperity

Garlic = protection

Olive (oil) = lust, healing, peace, protection, and fertility

GREEN THUMB

This is a great plant to add to the green witch's garden, as it offers protection to your garden and home. Basil needs to be in a location that gets six to eight hours of full sun daily. Soil should be evenly moist and well-drained. Plant seeds/seedlings about ¼-inch deep and ten to twelve inches apart. For small plants, space farther apart (about sixteen to twenty-four inches). They should grow about twelve to twenty-four inches in height. Harvest leaves when plants mature, and enjoy!

❧ Magical ❧ Mindfulness Tip

Sleep with a fresh twig of basil under your pillow to protect yourself from troubled dreams and to help achieve a peaceful sleep.

DID you KNOW?

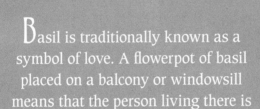

Basil is traditionally known as a
symbol of love. A flowerpot of basil
placed on a balcony or windowsill
means that the person living there is
available and ready for love.

(CATNIP)

(Nepeta)

Catmint is a beautiful herb that is dainty in appearance
but tough in character. It enchants both felines and
gardeners alike. Not only is it a mood stimulant for your
furry familiar, but it's also breathtaking when planted
in a cottage garden setting near roses. The foliage is
aromatic. The plants have sturdy stems with opposite
heart-shaped green leaves. The tiny tubular flowers are
often lavender or blue in color.

2 GREEN WITCHES SAYETH

"If you love your cat a lot, plant some catmint in a pot."

SIMPLE CAT LOVE MAGIC

(MAKES 1 TOY)

1 cotton sock (preferably a child's sock for its small size)
Dried catmint leaves
1 string
1 small bell (available at pet stores and craft shops)

Simply fill the sock with as much dried catmint as you can fit, then securely tie the end with a string. Tie a bell to the end of the string, and this will become your familiar's most bewitching toy!

THE PURRFECT DATE SPELL

Before a first date, chew on the fresh leaves of catmint to give yourself courage, boldness, and protection. Having fresh minty breath might also come in handy!

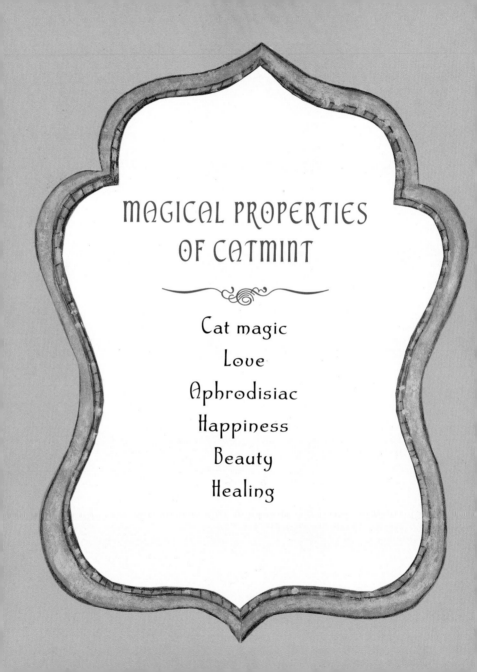

MAGICAL PROPERTIES OF CATMINT

Cat magic
Love
Aphrodisiac
Happiness
Beauty
Healing

GREEN THUMB

Keep a pot of catmint in a sunny spot with rich soil, and water regularly. It can be cut back in the autumn. Your familiar will enjoy chewing on the catmint, so be sure *never* to use pesticides or chemicals on or around it!

⟨ Magical ⟩
Mindfulness Tip

To calm your nerves, make a simple tea out of fresh or dried catmint. It's lovely taken at bedtime for a restful sleep.

DID YOU KNOW?

Catmint stimulates a cat's
pheromones which gives our familiars
an overwhelming sense of euphoria.
It is a protective plant that attracts
great luck and good spirits when
grown near your home. You can use
it with rose petals in love sachets.
When used as a tea, it can be good for
treating children's diarrhea and fever
or even as a mild sedative. Larger
catmint leaves can also be pressed
and used as bookmarks in magical
texts like this one!

DAISY

(EYE OF THE DAY)
(Chrysanthemum maximum)

Was there ever a sweeter flower than the simple and cheerful daisy with its sunshine center surrounded by exclamation points often of pure white? Supporting all this enchantment are bright green stems with lovely, almost fern-like leaves. Fairy folk are said to be especially fond of daisies!

2 GREEN WITCHES SAYETH

*"Faeries make sure your love is swell,
when you wear a daisy on your lapel."*

LOVES ME, LOVES ME NOT SPELL

Almost every child knows this classic! Pull up an entire daisy flower by the roots from your garden. Please never steal plants, for to do so shall bring bad luck. Holding the flower so it faces you, gently pull off one petal at a time. As you pull off each petal, recite "Loves me (one petal), loves me not (next petal) until there are no more petals. If the last petal ends on "Loves me," place the roots of the daisy under your pillow to help you dream of your beloved and draw them to you.

ATTRACTION SPELL

Simply thread a daisy through a buttonhole on your shirt or jacket to attract love. A daisy chain in your hair or a daisy tucked behind your ear works just as well. As you place the flowers, imagine yourself falling madly in love.

MAGICAL PROPERTIES OF DAISIES

Love

Lust

GREEN THUMB

Plant daisy seeds or plants in full sun. Soil should be moderately fertile and moist but well-drained. If you grow daisies directly from seed, expect blooms the following spring after one season's growth. You may also plant young plants from a nursery in spring for summer bloom. Most daisies are perennial and will return each spring for the Equinox.

DID YOU KNOW?

Norse witches consider daisies to be sacred to the Norse goddess Freya and use the flowers in childbirth ceremonies. Freya rides a chariot pulled by two cats (!). She represents love, fertility, beauty, battle, and death. Daisies are sometimes given to new mothers for luck.

❦ Magical ❧ Mindfulness Tip

Pick yourself a bouquet of daisies for your kitchen table to cheer and warm your heart every time you see them.

(ELVEN)

(Ulmus)

The elm is a beautiful deciduous tree whose pale green leaves are doubly toothed and lopsided at the base. In Celtic mythology, the elm tree is associated with the underworld. Many believe that elms grow at the entrances of passageways into the underworld. Thus, one should tread carefully when walking through a grove of elm trees!

2 GREEN WITCHES SAYETH

"Plant a protective elm by your door to bring love and safety forevermore."

SIMPLE LOVE SPELL

Carry a red velvet or velour sachet of elm flowers or small twigs with you to attract love. You may also grind the wood into a fine powder and burn it as incense in a small cauldron to bring love into your life.

ELM ATTRACTION AND PROTECTION

This is a simple one. Using seven young and nimble branches from an elm tree, cut them in pieces at least twenty-four inches or more—just make them uniform in size. Tie them together in a circle using string, wire, or a thin rope. Hang this elm wreath from your door to attract love as well as protect your home.

MAGICAL PROPERTIES
OF ELM

Love

Protection

GREEN THUMB

Bless your home by planting an elm tree in your garden. Plant in rich, composted soil in full to partial sun, and remember to leave enough room for the tree and the tree's roots to grow. Water regularly through the first year to establish your magical plant.

Magical Mindfulness Tip

Find a sunny day to sit against an adult elm tree. Bring a pad of plain paper. Ask the tree for advice about finding love. Sit quietly and see what thoughts come to mind. Write them down. This is how you channel tree wisdom. It may take a few tries before you get the "hang" of it!

DID YOU KNOW?

Long ago, the elm tree was better
known as the "elven" tree due to its
association and popularity with elves.
Elms are often found at the entrance
or portals to the fairy realms and
have always been considered trees
of protection. The American elm was
once a very common tree in the United
States but, thanks to Dutch elm
disease, the tree is now fairly rare.

(FEATHERFEW)

(Chrysanthemum parthenium)

Feverfew, with its daisy-like flowers and ferny foliage, has been used for centuries in spells and potions. Feverfew is a protection plant, and to carry it with you helps ward off sickness and accidents. It is also a strong herb for spiritual healing.

2 GREEN WITCHES SAYETH

"To find a love that's here to stay, make yourself a feverfew sachet!"

FEVERFEW LOVE SACHET

(MAKES 1 SACHET)

1 (2" × 4") pink sachet bag
2 sprigs fresh rosemary
1 acorn
1 small rose quartz stone
4 red rose petals
6 feverfew flowers

Fill your sachet with all ingredients. Every morning, place the sachet in your pocket. Once the spell has worked its magic and you have met your true love, you should return the contents of the sachet back to nature. (In doing so, you'll stay on the good side of the fairies. They want their items to be returned back to Mother Earth!)

MAGICAL PROPERTIES
OF FEVERFEW LOVE SACHET

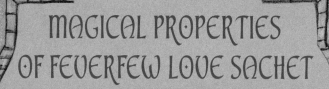

Feverfew = love and protection

Cotton = purity

Rosemary = love and passion

Acorn = sexual potency

Rose quartz = long-term love

Rose petals = love divination

FEVERFEW LOVE SPRAY

Cut up a few stems, leaves, and flowers of feverfew and boil in approximately 1 cup of full moon water (water that has been energized by the light of a full moon). Let steep for five minutes. Allow to cool, then strain the clear water into a spray bottle. Use it as a mist for love letters to add Venus's blessing to your message.

GREEN THUMB

Feverfew corresponds to Venus. To honor Venus, plant feverfew in full sun to light shade in a beautiful hand-decorated pot covered in hearts or anything that symbolizes love. If planting in the ground, you might want to find a heart-shaped rock to rest next to the plant. If you can't find a rock in this shape, simply paint a red heart on a rock. Well-drained soil is perfect for these plants. You can start seeds indoors in late winter or directly sow them in your garden after all danger of frost has passed. Germination takes ten to fourteen days.

DID YOU KNOW?

Feverfew was proven to be a safe and effective remedy for migraines in the seventeenth century by British herbalist John Gerard. It is most effective when used as a preventative. Frequent use of the herb over time is reported to reduce the severity of migraines, nausea, and vomiting. It has also been said to reduce inflammation and pain from arthritis. Early Romans used a concoction of feverfew flowers as a cosmetic wash.

Magical Mindfulness Tip

Cut yourself a posy of the dainty feverfew flowers to wear on your shirt to attract love and smiles throughout your day.

(PROTECTION FLOWER)

(Geraniaceae)

Geraniums tend to be richly colored five-petaled flowers with soft, fuzzy, heart-shaped leaves. We will mostly be talking about pelargoniums (commonly mistaken as geraniums) but there is also a temperate wildflower known as cranesbill that is also considered a geranium. Legend states that, in olden times, witches grew large patches of red geraniums around their cottages as a protection plant and that the geraniums would announce an approaching visitor by leaning in their direction.

2 GREEN WITCHES SAYETH

"Give geraniums to your lover true,
nd happiness will come to both of you."

LOVE POTPOURRI SPELL

To express an open heart to a new love, dry the flowers and leaves of different aromatic geraniums such as rose, peppermint, and lemon. Mix all together to create a lovely, scented potpourri and present it to your new love.

GERANIUM PROTECTION SPELL

Geraniums are very protective plants so the act of growing them in a windowsill or garden will ward off evil spirits and negative energy. We love our protective plants!

GREEN THUMB

Geraniums are simple plants to grow and they like full sun, rich soil, and good drainage. Water regularly. In colder seasons, bring them indoors to overwinter as a houseplant. Their ruling planet is Venus so for best results you may want to pot geraniums up at night when the planet Venus is visible.

❧ Magical ❧ Mindfulness Tip

Growing a pot of brightly colored geraniums at your doorway will not only attract love but will also cheer you as you come and go!

MAGICAL PROPERTIES OF GERANIUM

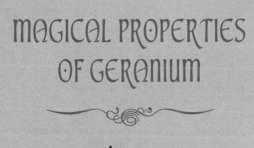

Love

Acceptance

Protection

Health

Fertility

Aura clearing

DID YOU KNOW?

Geraniums hail from South Africa where there are more than 250 species grown! Geraniums did not find their way to European gardens until the seventeenth century, and it wasn't until the eighteenth century that American gardeners were introduced to this bewitching plant. It is the national flower of Switzerland.

HYACINTH

(Hyacinthus)

Hyacinths with their sturdy stalks of brightly colored spring flowers are one of the loveliest and most strongly scented of all spring plants. A growing bulb placed in one's bedroom is said to stave off nightmares and anxiety dreams. The entire plant is toxic, so do not digest any part of it (also consider that having it in the house could be dangerous for nibbling pets).

2 GREEN WITCHES SAYETH

"Hyacinth given as an aromatic bouquet, will make your true love stay whether straight or gay!"

WINNING OVER A NEW LOVE SPELL

Simply present your beloved with a fresh bouquet of hyacinths. It's sure to make them swoon.

HEAL A BROKEN HEART SPELL

Carry dried flowers in a sachet or locket to heal a broken heart.

MAGICAL PROPERTIES OF HYACINTH

Love
Abundance
Happiness
Charm
Play
Joy
Protection

GREEN THUMB

Plant these magical bulbs in full sun to part shade four inches deep and three inches apart. In more northerly climes, plant six to eight inches deep. Grow in well-drained, moderately fertile soil. They grow well where winters are cold.

❧ Magical ❧ Mindfulness Tip

Go to the nursery and bring home a pot of hyacinths to fill your home or workplace with the scent of spring. Do this as a treat just for you. If you have pets, keep the plants up high where they cannot chew on them. We don't want any sick familiars!

DID YOU KNOW?

In ancient Greek mythology, Apollo, the sun god, and Zephyr, the god of the west wind, found themselves in competition for the attention of a dashing young Spartan prince named Hyakinthos. Legend has it that one day Apollo was teaching Hyakinthos how to throw a discus, and in a jealous rage, Zephyr blew a giant gust of wind so strong that it caused the discus to strike Hyakinthos in the head, killing him instantly. Flowers grew from where his blood was spilled on the ground and a mourning Apollo named the flower hyacinth. To this day, hyacinths are known as symbols of jealousy and sorrow. Due to the romantic connection between Apollo and Hyakinthos, this flower is often used in spells to attract same-sex love.

(GRANDMOTHER'S HAIR)

(Castilleja)

Indian paintbrush flowers are native to California and come in a mix of red, orange, yellow, pink, or purple. The colorful parts of the flowers are actually modified leaves made to attract pollinators. The flowers themselves are tiny and yellow or whitish-green and are densely packed to form a spike. They bloom all summer long and brighten the low-water garden.

2 GREEN WITCHES SAYETH

"Carrying Indian paintbrush in your purse,
will attract a lover for better or worse."

SIMPLE LOVE SPELL

Place several Indian paintbrush blossoms in a sachet along with a green jade stone and some morning glory seeds. Carry the sachet in your pocket or purse to attract love.

☙ Magical ❧
Mindfulness Tip

Though Indian paintbrush may be a difficult plant to grow, it's not impossible. Add other native plants around your Indian paintbrushes. Planting them will benefit the wildlife and pollinators in your area. Creating a little habitat, whether in a flowerbox or a garden, will lighten your heart as you observe the bees and butterflies flitting happily around your plants.

MAGICAL PROPERTIES OF SIMPLE LOVE SPELL

Indian paintbrush = love and
a colorful relationship

Green jade stone = harmony

Morning glory seeds = tenacity

GREEN THUMB

Indian paintbrush is not a simple plant to propagate. It is a hemiparasite, which means that it needs to feed off the roots of a host plant to grow. However, it will not harm the host. If growing by seed, be sure to plant it next to a host plant. We have done this successfully by planting it next to a native Island Snapdragon (*Gambelia speciose*) and blue-eyed grass (*Schizachyrium scoparium*). They do not transplant well, so sow seeds exactly where you want them to grow. The plant needs well-draining soil, a sunny spot, and a locale where winters are warm. In a Mediterranean climate, we recommend planting the seeds during the second harvest festival of Mabon in autumn.

DID YOU KNOW?

In his book *Legend of the Indian Paintbrush*, author Tomie dePaola tells the Native American legend of a particularly small boy who was too little and weak to play with the other boys so he took up painting. He painted wonderful pictures of his family and his world. His paintings were much admired by all who saw them. One day, the young boy decided he wanted to capture the unique beauty of a sunset but, try as he might, he just could not get his paintings to capture the glory. The young boy asked for guidance from the Great Spirit. The Great Spirit came to the boy in a dream and directed him to where he would find paintbrushes capable of reproducing the colors he desired. With his new brushes, he painted a masterpiece and then scattered the spent brushes around the meadow. In the morning, he was delighted to find that his used paintbrushes had taken root and sprouted the flowers we now call Indian paintbrush.

JASMINE

(Moonlight on the Grove)
(Jasminum)

Magical jasmine is deservedly known for its strong
sensual scent. Surprisingly, such a gorgeous aroma
comes from small, modest white flowers. Poet's jasmine
blooms on an aggressive vine, and night-blooming
jasmine grows as a tall bush. Jasmine tends to thrive in
warm climates or as a houseplant in a sunny spot. Once
you've smelled its bewitching scent, you will be hooked!
Added bonus: Jasmine is not toxic to pets.

2 GREEN WITCHES SAYETH

"A jasmine bath for you, shall bring a lover true."

BATH SALTS SPELL FOR ATTRACTING LOVE

(MAKES ABOUT 2½ CUPS)

2 cups Epsom salts
2 teaspoons organic extra virgin olive oil
5–10 drops jasmine essential oil
1 dropper (about 16 mg) CBD oil
¼ cup sea salt
¼ cup baking soda

Add all ingredients to a large mixing bowl and stir to combine.

Add 2 to 4 tablespoons of bath salts to a tub of running water and focus your intention of attracting love into your life while enjoying a *scents*ational soak!

Store mixture in a glass jar with a lid.

❧ Magical ❧ Mindfulness Tip

Jasmine bath salts will not only attract love; they will also leave you smelling like a woodland fairy! Do this for yourself when you need to unwind.

MAGICAL PROPERTIES OF BATH SALTS SPELL

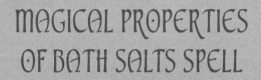

Jasmine = love, tranquility, attraction, prosperity, and prophetic dreams

CBD oil (marijuana) = love, healing, and calming

Olive (oil) = lust, healing, peace, protection, and fertility

GREEN THUMB

All types of jasmine are subtropical to tropical plants, but for more northerly witches, they can be indoor houseplants. Plant jasmine in compost-rich soil in a sunny to partially sunny location and water regularly. Plants can be cut back hard in the winter to promote a more compact size. Before transplanting, set a full watering can under a full moon. Wait until the next day and use this water on the plant's roots right after planting.

❧ Magical ☙ Mindfulness Tip

The gods of love (Cupid, Eros, and Kama) are always represented with a bow and arrow tipped with jasmine flowers in order to pierce a target's heart with desire. Jasmine is thought to have been brought across the Red Sea from Persia into Egypt in 1,000 BCE for propagation.

(Kalanchoe)

Kalanchoe is a dark green succulent with scalloped leaves. It is a long-living perennial that is best grown indoors as a houseplant. Its bloom time is bewitchingly long and comes in a huge array of bright, tropical colors.

2 GREEN WITCHES SAYETH

"Kalanchoe in a pot by your love's door, assures their devotion forevermore."

KALANCHOE LOVE SPELL

This is a simple spell but, as with all spells, the real power comes with the intention you have as you carry it out. Start with a trip to the local nursery, ideally one with a greenhouse. Such visits are always a salve for one's soul. Pick out a kalanchoe plant in your favorite color and a clay pot to plant it in. Fill your pot with topsoil and your new plant. We recommend painting the pot in bright, tropical reds, apricots, and pinks to further attract love. Gift to someone special.

❧ Magical ❧ Mindfulness Tip

Get yourself a pot of pink flowering kalanchoe for your bathroom window to provide you protection and a cheerful beginning and end to each day.

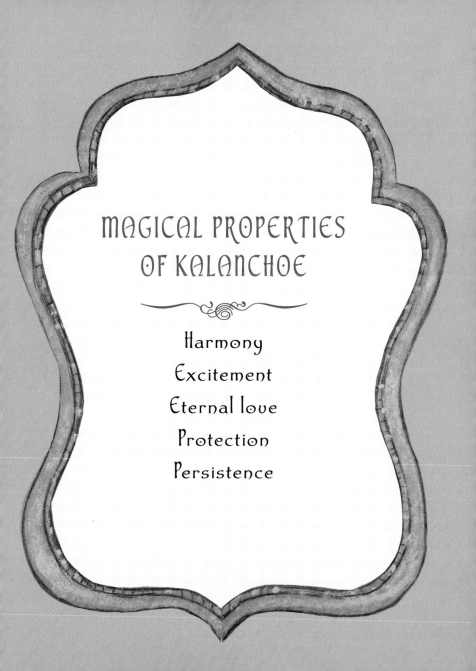

MAGICAL PROPERTIES OF KALANCHOE

Harmony
Excitement
Eternal love
Protection
Persistence

GREEN THUMB

Kalanchoe needs regular water and very good drainage. Place in sun to partial sun. Succulent kalanchoe can grow outdoors only where winters are mild and warm. It also makes a nice houseplant and is best grown indoors in a clay pot. *Beware!* Some species of kalanchoes are toxic to familiars. If you have cats in your house, you can prevent them from chewing kalanchoe leaves by sprinkling cayenne pepper over the plant or putting it somewhere they won't be tempted to nibble.

DID YOU KNOW?

Kalanchoe is a very popular plant during Lunar New Year celebrations. In China, it is said to bring wealth and prosperity. The plant is also called "thousands and millions of red and purple." The plant was imported to Europe from China around 1930 and bred by German seed merchant Robert Blossfeld.

LAVENDER

(Elf Leaf)

(Lavandula)

Lavender is perhaps one of the most enchanting of all flowers due largely to its perfume and soft beauty. It is best known as an aromatherapy plant for its calming properties. The delicate and fuzzy-leaved herb with its long purple spikes of tiny flowers is Mediterranean in origin and has been used in love spells for centuries. It is said that men respond most strongly to its scent.

2 GREEN WITCHES SAYETH

*"Soothing lavender in a candle,
will bring all the love that you can handle."*

BURNING LOVE
CANDLE SPELL

(MAKES 2 CANDLES)

Prepare a lovely meal for your intended and use this lavender love candle as a romantic centerpiece on your table. Never leave lit candles unattended!

3 cups water
4 cups soy flakes
2 wicks with metal base
2 (8-ounce) glass jars
2 large clothespins
30 drops lavender essential oil, divided
2 teaspoons dried lavender, divided

In a double boiler, bring the water to a boil. Once the water is boiling, reduce heat to a simmer and add in the soy flakes. With a spoon that you do not use for cooking, stir the soy flakes until they are reduced to a liquid. This process can take about 5 minutes.

Once the soy is liquified, remove from heat and dip the metal ends of the wicks into the wax. Place the ends in the center of each candle jar, pressing the metal ends down with a skewer or chopstick until set. The wax acts like a glue to secure the metal end at the bottom of each candle jar.

Once the metal end is set in the wax, gently straighten the wick and secure it at the mouth of the jar with a clothespin resting on the jar. Slowly pour the wax into each jar. Add 15 drops of lavender essential oil to each jar (this is done now to avoid burning the oils during the cooking process).

Add 1 teaspoon of dried lavender to each jar. Using the skewer or chopstick, gently stir the wax.

Let the candles sit for 24 hours. Once set, remove the clothespins and trim the top of the wicks to 1 inch in length.

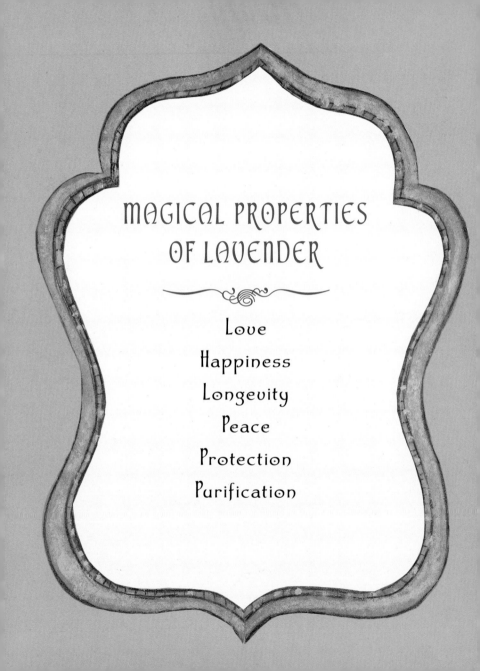

MAGICAL PROPERTIES OF LAVENDER

Love
Happiness
Longevity
Peace
Protection
Purification

❈ Magical ❈
Mindfulness Tip

Treat yourself to a warm bath with lavender bath salts
before bed for a relaxing night's sleep.

GREEN THUMB

Bewitching lavender grows well outdoors in a warm Mediterranean climate. Plant in well-drained soil. As you fill the soil in around the roots, ask the local elves to bless your garden. Lavender does not need a rich soil or fertilizer. Place in a sunny spot near a path or doorway where the scent can be enjoyed. After blooming, trim the plant to keep its shape.

DID YOU KNOW?

People have been using lavender for well over 2,500 years. Not only was lavender used as a remedy during the Great Plague of London, but ancient Egyptians also used lavender for mummification and as a perfume. Ancient Romans washed clothes in lavender and dried their clothing in the sun on lavender bushes.

MEADOWSWEET

(BRIDE OF THE MEADOW)

(Filipendula ulmaria)

Meadowsweet, or mead wort, is a perennial herb which craves moist soil. The dainty white blooms resemble snowflakes and have a lovely almond scent. It's a wonderful addition to any witch's cottage garden. People have used the herb to treat colds, gout, and heartburn. Magically, meadowsweet was considered by the druids to be one of the most sacred herbs. It is known to attract love, happiness, and peace. Place meadowsweet on your altar when conjuring love spells for more success.

2 GREEN WITCHES SAYETH

*"Carry meadowsweet when we meet,
and peace and love shall be our treat."*

SIMPLE PEACEMAKING SPELL

Sprinkle meadowsweet blossoms around the bedroom to ensure peace between you and your love.

PAIN-FREE LOVE TEA

(SERVES 2)

Drink this minty meadowsweet tea to promote a love without drama.

2 cups water
1 bunch fresh meadowsweet flowers or 2 teaspoons dried
1 bunch (about 1 cup) coarsely chopped fresh mint leaves
1–2 tablespoons organic maple syrup or organic sugar

In a medium saucepan, combine water, meadowsweet, and mint and bring to a boil.

Remove from heat and let steep for 10 minutes to reach potency. Strain through a fine mesh sieve into a teapot or container. Discard solids into your compost bin.

Mix in maple syrup or sugar for a sweeter tea.

ℛ Magical ℛ Mindfulness Tip

Though this lovely tea is meant to be shared with your love, you can also brew it for yourself. It will have a calming effect after a stressful day.

MAGICAL PROPERTIES OF PAIN-FREE LOVE TEA

Meadowsweet = love, peace, happiness, and divination

Mint = protection, healing, love, and luck

Maple (syrup) = love and healing

Sugar = healing and sweetness

GREEN THUMB

Plant meadowsweet in a partially shaded area that has well-drained soil with lots of compost. Add mulch such as untreated bark chips around the plants to help the soil retain water. Make sure the mulch doesn't actually touch the plants. Water regularly during the first year, providing it with 1 inch of water weekly from spring until fall. When harvesting meadowsweet, say once, "Beautiful meadowsweet, bring love to me. This is my wish. So mote it be."

DID YOU KNOW?

The herb meadowsweet contains a small amount of salicylic acid which makes it a natural and effective pain reliever. Unlike aspirin, it doesn't upset one's digestive system. The herb contains mucilaginous qualities that are said to soften the salicylic acid's effect on the stomach. Meadowsweet tea has a lovely almond flavor.

NARCISSUS

(Narcissus)

Narcissus originated from southwest Europe and is grown from bulbs. This spring-blooming plant features strappy leaves and a stem holding cup-and-saucer-shaped flowers known for their bewitching sweet scent. It is known as a symbol of spring. All parts of this plant are toxic and are never to be ingested. Magically, putting a bouquet of narcissus in a vase is said to bring abundance to your home. Gift them for good luck!

2 GREEN WITCHES SAYETH

"A bouquet of narcissus, you see,
proves my love is for no one but me."

SELF-LOVE SPELL

**Hold a bouquet of narcissus, face yourself in the mirror,
and recite the following:**

"I pledge and do expect,
To treat myself with self-respect.
I shall learn to love myself,
Deeper than anyone else.
I promise myself to be true,
And trust that I'll know what to do.
I know that I am enough,
Even when times are tough.
This vow I make to me,
so mote it be."

MAGICAL PROPERTIES OF NARCISSUS

Self-love
Confidence
Hope
Inner peace

ᘓ Magical ᘔ
Mindfulness Tip

Narcissus is the flower of self-love—and there's absolutely nothing wrong with that! As a present to yourself, grow narcissus indoors and breathe it in every time you walk past. Let the scent be a symbol of the love and respect you have for yourself. Remember to keep it away from nibbling familiars.

GREEN THUMB

Fill a shallow container (such as a vintage ceramic bowl with no drainage) with pebbles, marbles, or decorative stones. Pack your bulbs into the bowl and push them down into the stones so that the tips face upright. Add water until it just covers the bottom of the bulbs. After planting, keep the bulbs in a cool, dark place for several weeks until the roots take hold and shoots start to sprout. Then, place the container in a cool, sunny location. In four to six weeks, you'll see tiny blossoms on the flower stems. Place blooming plants in a spot where you can enjoy their sweet scent. For a witchy touch, grow your narcissus in front of a mirror.

If you live in a warm area that doesn't freeze in winter, you may transfer bulbs outside once they have finished blooming. Cut back dead leaves before planting. They will magically return in the spring.

DID YOU KNOW?

In ancient Greek mythology, Narcissus was a beautiful hunter and all who gazed upon him fell in love with him. However, this admiration from others was only met with disdain by Narcissus. Once the Oread nymph Echo caught sight of him she fell in love right away and tried to hug him but Narcissus pushed her away and told her to leave him alone. Echo was brokenhearted and eventually wilted away until all that remained of her was an echo.

Nemesis, the goddess of revenge, learned of Echo's fate and vowed to punish Narcissus. She led the beautiful man to a pool where he saw his reflection and fell madly in love with it. When he realized it was only a reflection and that his love with the man looking back could never be, he tragically killed himself.

ORANGE

(Love Fruit)

(Citrus x sinensis)

The orange is a medium-sized flowering evergreen tree. Though the small white flowers aren't very showy, they make up for it with their dreamy perfume. These flowers are pollinated and become the beloved sweet orange fruit. The tree is branching and rounded in shape and grows best in a Mediterranean climate. A freeze would be deadly. Its wild ancestor is believed to have come from the southeastern region of China. The orange has been in cultivation since the 1600s.

2 GREEN WITCHES SAYETH

"Love, I summon thee with an orange cake. With every bite, your heart I shall take."

ORANGE YOU GLAD MAGICAL CAKE

(SERVES 4–6)

Repeat the rhyme on page 131 in your mind as you prepare this magical cake and enjoy with your love!

CAKE

3 cups flour
1 cup organic sugar
¼ teaspoon salt
1 teaspoon baking powder
1 teaspoon baking soda
¼ cup grapeseed oil
2 cups organic orange juice
1 teaspoon pure vanilla extract
2 teaspoons pure orange extract
Orange zest from 1 organic orange
Organic blueberries
Candied Violet Flowers (page 199)

FROSTING

2 sticks dairy-free margarine at
   room temperature
3 cups powdered sugar
2 tablespoons dairy-free cashew
   milk
⅛ teaspoon salt
1 teaspoon vanilla extract

Continued on next page

MAKE THE CAKE

Preheat oven to 350°F. Grease 2 (9-inch) cake pans and sprinkle with a dusting of flour.

Mix together flour, sugar, salt, baking powder, and baking soda in one large bowl. In another large bowl, mix together the oil, orange juice, and extracts.

Whisk approximately 1 cup of the dry ingredients into the wet ingredients. Then, stir in remaining dry ingredients.

Pour cake batter into cake pan(s).

Bake for 25 minutes, or until a toothpick inserted in the center comes out clean. Let both layers of cake cool completely before assembling, ideally overnight in the fridge.

MAKE THE FROSTING

With a hand mixer, beat margarine until whipped. Slowly add in the powdered sugar and beat until fluffy.

Mix in cashew milk, salt, and vanilla.

The mixture should be thick and easy to spread. Add more powdered sugar if too thin. You should end up with 1½ cups frosting.

ASSEMBLY

Once cooled, use a long, serrated knife to trim the tops of both cake layers to make flat surfaces.

Evenly cover the top of the first layer with about 1 cup frosting. Spread the frosting so it extends just beyond the edges of the cake. After the top is covered, press in a couple dozen fresh blueberries.

Carefully place the second cake layer cut side down on top of the bottom cake. Press it into the first cake gently to make it level.

Cover the top of the cake with a thin layer of frosting and refrigerate cake for 15 minutes.

Using a large spatula, generously coat the chilled cake with the rest of your frosting and garnish with orange zest, the rest of your blueberries, and Candied Violet Flowers.

MAGICAL PROPERTIES OF ORANGE YOU GLAD MAGICAL CAKE

Orange = love, luck,
and fertility

Blueberry = protection, beauty,
and peace

Vanilla = love and lust

Cashew (milk) = prosperity

Violets = love, luck, and healing

Sugar = sweetness and healing

❧ Magical ❧ Mindfulness Tip

Eat an orange and let the peels dry out on a sunny windowsill. Carry the peelings in a simple sachet to give your courage a boost when you need it. You may also use a whole orange to make a pomander to freshen the scent of a room by spiking an orange with cloves, lavender, and rosemary sprigs. Place pomander on your nightstand for sweet dreams.

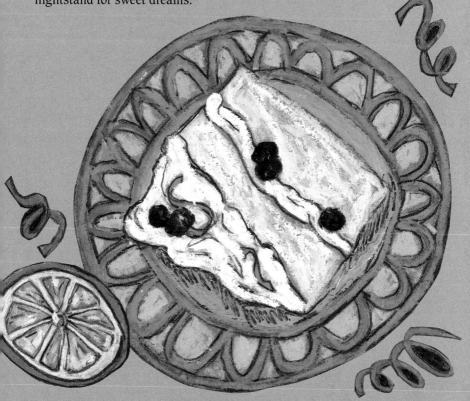

GREEN THUMB

Citrus trees need warmth to fruit and are typically grown in areas with mild winters. Plant in fast-draining rich soil. Ideally, citrus trees need moist (but not soggy) soil. You never want your orange tree sitting in water. Use compost to maintain soil moisture. Fertilize several times through the growing season. If leaves yellow, they may be lacking in nitrogen, so you will need to fertilize. Hera the Greek goddess rules over orange. As a tribute to her, plant a ring of irises in a circle four feet around your orange tree.

DID YOU KNOW?

Orange fruit were first recorded in history in China as early as 314 BCE. Louis XIV of France was so enamored by the sweet fruit that he built a fabulous royal orangerie designed by Jules Hardouin-Mansart at the Palace of Versailles. The Versailles orangerie was actually built even before the construction on the Palace of Versailles had begun. Citrus was considered highly fashionable for the rich nobility of the time, and to have an orangerie was the height of extravagance!

(Devil's Oatmeal)
(Petroselinum crispum)

Parsley, with its fresh scent and taste, sprays of dainty flowers, and delicate bright green leaves, has been a favored herb since ancient times. It was first used popularly in England in the Middle Ages. It is typically grown as a biennial. The plant will die once it seeds.

2 Green Witches Sayeth

"To encourage passion and lust, carry sprigs of parsley and trust."

LOVER'S LUSTY SIMPLE SALAD

(MAKES 4 SERVINGS)

1 large organic red onion, thinly sliced
1 teaspoon organic sugar
3 tablespoons organic olive oil
1 tablespoon balsamic vinegar
1 teaspoon organic maple syrup
4 cups (lightly packed) fresh flat-leaf parsley leaves with tender stems
¼ cup pomegranate seeds
Salt and pepper, to taste

Toss onion in a medium bowl with sugar, oil, vinegar, and maple syrup. Let sit for 5 minutes.

Just before serving, toss in parsley and pomegranate seeds. Season with salt and pepper, to taste.

SOOTHING PARSLEY TEA

Steep fresh parsley in a cup of hot water, strain, and drink as a treat for yourself. It is high in antioxidants and is a good source of vitamin c. It is also said to prevent kidney stones when taken regularly.

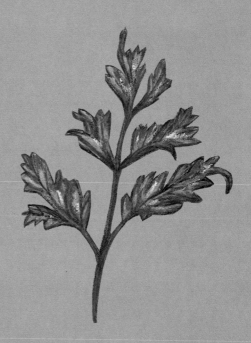

MAGICAL PROPERTIES OF LOVER'S LUSTY SIMPLE SALAD

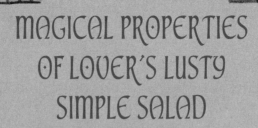

Parsley = lust, purification, and protection

Pomegranate = fertility and wealth

Onion = protection

Sugar = sweetness and healing

Olive (oil) = peace and friendship

Maple (syrup) = love and healing

GREEN THUMB

Plant seeds in fertile and loamy soil with good drainage, no deeper than half an inch. Parsley does best in a cool and sunny area. Keep soil evenly moist until germination. Water plants when soil is dry to the touch. You may harvest leaves for cooking or simply let them bloom. Parsley is a lovely bloomer and attracts butterflies, which naturally bring magic into any garden.

SIMPLE PARSLEY SPELL

Carry parsley clippings in a sachet or make a posey to pin to your clothing to attract passion into your life.

DID YOU KNOW?

In ancient Greek mythology, parsley first sprouted from the spilled blood of Archemorus, who was slain by a dragon. Ancient Greeks believed that parsley was sacred. Greek soldiers fed parsley to their horses to give them strength. They also placed garlands of parsley on winning athletes as well as on tombs of the dead. Parsley can be planted at a grave site for remembrance.

2 GREEN WITCHES SAYETH

"Queen Anne's lace, so delicate and fine,
will reinvigorate a love dried on the vine."

QUEEN ANNE'S LACE

(Daucus carota)

These beauties are tall (up to three feet) and grow gloriously wild in fields and meadows all over North America. The "flower" is comprised of thousands of tiny white flowers with lacey flat-topped clusters surrounding a dark purple center flower. Like many of our favorite plants, the leaves are very ferny.

QUEEN ANNE'S LACE PURIFICATION

This flower symbolizes the purity of intent in your love spells. Place a big bouquet of it on your altar before conjuring and let Queen Anne's Lace ensure a pure spell!

❧ Magical ❧
Mindfulness Tip

We highly recommend adding Queen Anne's Lace flowers to your bath. Use them fresh or dry them for later when you could use a wintertime soak! It will make your skin glow.

QUEEN ANNE'S LACE JELLY

(MAKES 4 CUPS)

Reinvigorate your relationship with this recipe!

4 cups water
2 cups fresh Queen Anne's lace flowers, stems trimmed and composted
¼ cup organic lemon juice
1 package powdered pectin
3 cups organic cane sugar

Bring water to a boil. Place flowers in a bowl, pour the water over flowers, and cover. Let infuse overnight. Strain and discard solids into your compost bin.

Pour strained mixture into a small saucepan and bring to a boil. Stir in lemon juice, pectin, and sugar. Continue stirring and boil for 1 more minute. Remove from heat and skim the foam off the top.

Let cool slightly and pour into 4 (8-ounce) jelly jars. Put the jars in a boiling water bath for 10 minutes.

Serve on toast for your love to add sparks to a fading romance.

MAGICAL PROPERTIES
OF QUEEN ANNE'S LACE JELLY

Queen Anne's Lace = aphrodisiac,
psychic abilities, fertility,
and intuition

Lemon (juice) = friendship

Sugar = healing and sweetness

GREEN THUMB

Due to its ability to spread, many consider Queen Anne's Lace to be a weed. But what a gorgeous weed this delicate cottagey-looking plant is! Simply spread the seeds over the area where you would like your plants to grow. As you do, say out loud, "Queen Anne's Lace, so full of grace, make this garden a magical place." This flower is a biennial, which means it often takes two years for it to bloom. Expect ferny foliage in the first season and beautiful intricate umbrellas of dainty white flowers in the second. If you don't want them to spread, simply deadhead before they go to seed. You'll want plenty of flowers for making your jelly!

DID YOU KNOW?

Queen Anne of England, the flower's namesake, once pricked her finger while tatting lace. Flecks of blood sprinkled onto her delicate work, leaving dark purple spots in their wake, similar to the speck of purple found at the center of every Queen Anne's Lace flower.

ROSE

(THE QUEEN OF FLOWERS)

(Rosa)

It is clear why the rose is considered the Queen of Flowers! Her strong, thorny constitution is topped off by beautifully colored, silky flowers, sometimes mimicking the look of a half cabbage in their shape and lushness. Roses, beyond all flowers, are often known for their romantic scents. The smell of a fruity scented rose is one of my earliest memories. Roses have been seducing humankind throughout the ages. Rose flowers range in size from small to very large. The rose plant's fleshy fruit, known as a hip, can be eaten raw or used in teas and is high in vitamin C.

2 GREEN WITCHES SAYETH

*"Add roses to your bath
for a love that will last."*

QUEEN OF

ROSE PETAL LOVE SOAP

(MAKES 4–6 BARS)

2 teaspoons dried rose petals (ideally from your own
  pesticide-free garden)
1 pound clear vegetable glycerin melt and pour soap
½ teaspoon sweet almond oil
½ teaspoon vitamin E oil
1 teaspoon rose essential oil
Silicone soap molds
Fresh rose petals (optional)

Using a mortar and pestle, grind up the dried rose petals and set aside.
Using a large knife, cut the soap into cubes, then melt the soap in a
double boiler. When the soap has melted, remove the double boiler from
the heat. Add the ground rose petals and stir gently to incorporate, then
stir in the almond and vitamin E oils.

Pour the soap into a glass measuring cup and stir in the rose essential
oil. Pour your soap into silicone soap molds. Let soap cool and harden
fully, then remove from the molds.

Enjoy your soap in a bath! Add in fresh rose petals if desired for
a romantic soak. This soap can also be used as a refreshing facial
cleanser.

MAGICAL PROPERTIES OF ROSE PETAL LOVE SOAP

Rose = love, luck, protection,
healing, and love divination

Almond (oil) = prosperity
and wisdom

❦ Magical ❧
Mindfulness Tip

Make a simple potpourri as a wonderful aromatherapy for yourself. Simply combine dried red roses, dried rose buds of various colors, dried lavender, and dried cloves for a scent that will ease your soul and encourage happy dreams when placed at your bedside. Add a rose quartz to the top of this potpourri to boost its loving and calming power.

GREEN THUMB

Luckily, there are various kinds of roses that can be grown in many different climates. Plant in well-draining rich soil in a sunny spot where your rose bush's roots will not have to compete with the roots of other shrubs or trees. Water your rose regularly, especially through hot and dry summers. It is a good idea to mulch around the base of the roses to help maintain soil moisture. Roses thrive when regularly fertilized. Many roses bloom more profusely when pruned way back in early spring. Cut out dead and weak older growth. Planting rose bushes in groups of three, in a triangle pattern, can really make for a bold effect in the garden. To honor the goddess Aphrodite, place a piece of coral in the center of your three rose bushes. Aphrodite will bless you and your roses.

DID YOU KNOW?

In Greek mythology, the red rose was created by Aphrodite. The goddess fell in love with the hunky god Adonis. One day she warned him not to hunt too deep inside the forest and to fear any animal that did not fear him. Adonis ignored her warning and was killed by a wild boar deep in the woods. Legend has it that red roses grew from the ground where Aphrodite's tears mixed with the blood of Adonis.

2 GREEN WITCHES SAYETH

*"Strawberry, strawberry, so red and sweet,
I'll steal your heart with this delicious treat."*

(THE FOOD OF LOVE)

(Fragaria x ananassa)

Strawberries are low-growing perennial plants. They produce beautiful red and sometimes white fruits on runners. They have tiny edible seeds which appear all over the surface of the fruit. The berries are soft and sweet when ripe. Strawberries are packed with lots of antioxidants and more vitamin C than an orange, and are a great source of manganese and potassium. Eating strawberries is especially good for healthy hair! The fruit of the strawberry, when shared with one's crush, can help win their heart.

MY BELOVED'S STRAWBERRY TART

(SERVES 4)

1 premade vegan pie dough
1 pound fresh organic strawberries, halved and stems removed
3 tablespoons organic sugar, divided
2 tablespoons cornstarch
1 tablespoon organic lemon juice
1 tablespoon almond milk

Thaw pie dough for 1 to 2 hours at room temperature, then preheat oven to
425°F. Place the strawberries in a medium bowl and sprinkle with 2 tablespoons
sugar, cornstarch, and lemon juice. Toss to coat and let stand for 10 minutes.
Place the dough on a large sheet of parchment paper on your counter. Using a
rolling pin, roll out the crust to 13 inches round. Place the strawberry mixture
in the center of the dough and evenly distribute. Fold
about 1½ inches of the dough edges toward the
center, covering strawberries slightly along
the edge. This will give your tart a rustic
look. Brush plant milk over the top of
your crust. Sprinkle the top crust around
the edges with the remaining sugar. Bake
until the crust is golden brown, about 25
minutes. Let stand for 10 minutes. Serve to
your beloved!

⊂ Magical ∾
Mindfulness Tip

To help cleanse your aura, burn strawberry incense while cleaning or tidying up your home. As you light the incense, say "Into the smoke I release all negative energy."

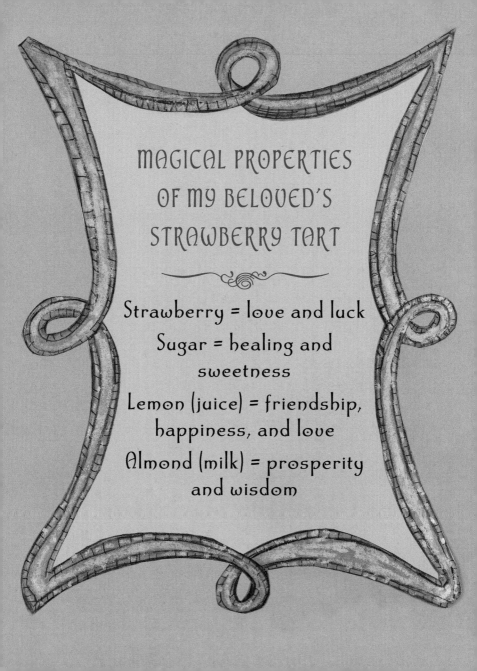

MAGICAL PROPERTIES OF MY BELOVED'S STRAWBERRY TART

Strawberry = love and luck

Sugar = healing and sweetness

Lemon (juice) = friendship, happiness, and love

Almond (milk) = prosperity and wisdom

GREEN THUMB

Strawberry plants are perennials with a life span of approximately three years. Select a sunny spot for your strawberry bed that has moist, well-drained soil. Add lots of organic compost. Plant June-bearing strawberries in early spring in rows four feet apart. Plants should be placed about two feet apart, as they will spread. For day-neutral and everbearing types of strawberries, clip off the runners and do not allow them to spread. Maintain the original plants for better fruit. The strawberry's element is water. To honor this and add some magic to your garden, place sea shells, corals, blue marbles, quartz, and driftwood among your plants.

Strawberries are one of the healthiest foods we can eat, as they are a rich source of antioxidants. Their high vitamin C content supports a strong immune system. If you eat strawberries after a rich meal, they will help with blood sugar regulation. They are wonderful for heart health due to their very high content of berry anthocyanins. Strawberries are said to help with weight management by satisfying sweet-tooth cravings. The first propagated strawberries were grown in France in the late eighteenth century.

(Tulipa)

Tulips are spring-blooming perennials. Their flowers are generally large, brightly colored, and quite showy, forming a large "cup" with dark blotches on the insides of the petals. The plants have pale green leaves. Red tulips are most strongly associated with love.

2 GREEN WITCHES SAYETH

"Your love spells will never falter, when tulips are placed upon your altar."

TULIP MAGIC

$\mathcal{A}$ny spell you do will be strengthened by placing a bouquet or pot of blooming tulips upon your altar. Based on the type of spell you're conjuring, you will want to use tulips of the appropriate color. For instance, yellow for happiness; green for new beginnings; pink for luck; apricot for friendship; and of course red for your love spells.

PROTECT MY
HEART TULIP OIL

We have created this magical oil to beautify your skin and help protect your heart from love gone awry.

6 cups full moon water
½ cup fresh red tulip petals
½ cup fresh rose petals
1 cup jojoba oil
3 drops vitamin E oil

In a saucepan, bring moon water to a boil, then remove from heat. Using a mortar and pestle, crush tulip petals, then crush rose petals. Empty all petals into a jar with a lid, then add in jojoba oil and vitamin E oil. Seal jar and set in pan of hot moon water. Leave for 24 hours, then strain the oil through a cheesecloth. Pour the clear oil back into your jar.

This oil will last up to 30 days if stored in a cool, dry place.

⊱ Magical ⊰
Mindfulness Tip

To calm and center yourself, grab a notepad or blank paper and colored pens and pencils and try your hand at sketching some beautiful tulip flowers. Do not worry about how good your drawing is. Simply notice how making yourself concentrate on the magical shapes and colors of tulips can be so relaxing!

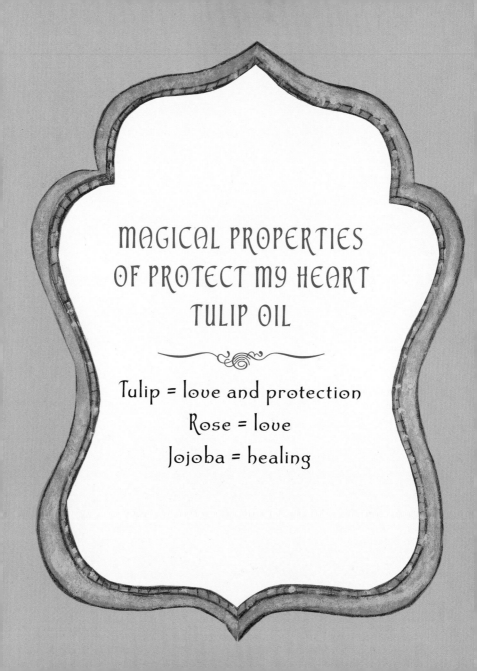

MAGICAL PROPERTIES OF PROTECT MY HEART TULIP OIL

Tulip = love and protection

Rose = love

Jojoba = healing

GREEN THUMB

If you live in an area with cold winters, you will be able to grow magical tulips (they need a frost to survive). Plant in full sun in rich, sandy soil. Tulips need good drainage; they will rot if too wet. Plant bulbs three times as deep as the bulbs are wide. The best time to plant in the garden is autumn during the Harvest Moon.

DID YOU KNOW?

There was a really intense tulip mania happening in the Netherlands in the seventeenth century. The market for tulips in that country created the first speculative market and a subsequent crash. A tulip called the Semper Augustus, white streaked with red stripes, was considered the most beautiful and rare of all tulips at the time. At the height of the mania, this bulb was priced at 10,000 guilders (or $5,700). With that kind of money, one could have purchased a mansion at the time!

(THE MOTHER GODDESS TREE)

(Magnolia tripetala)

Magnolias are a very ancient species which developed on Earth long before bees evolved. To this day, they are pollinated by beetles. Fossils of magnolias have been found dating back twenty million years! Magnolias are spreading shrubs or trees and boast a strong scent. Their flowers range in color, including pink, white, purple, yellow, and green. They bloom in spring. Cone-shaped fruits are produced in autumn.

2 GREEN WITCHES SAYETH

"Sit under an umbrella magnolia tree, for the protection of your true love and thee."

LOVE SPELL JAR

To help attract a love with the qualities you most admire.

1 pen with red ink
1 piece of paper
½ cup white sugar
1+ pink or red roses
3+ lavender sprigs
1 rose quartz stone
1 (4-inch) magnolia stem
1 (12-inch) piece pink or red ribbon

Using pen and paper, write down the qualities of your ideal partner and be as specific or as general as you like. Then, add white sugar, for a sweet love, to a jar with a lid. On top of the sugar, anchor at least one rose and at least three lavender sprigs. (Optional: Add a rose quartz to amplify the love vibes!) Place a small magnolia branch in the center of the jar. Tuck in your paper, seal it up, and tie a ribbon around the top of the jar. Set this jar in a cool, dark space in your bedroom.

MAGICAL PROPERTIES OF LOVE SPELL JAR

Magnolia (stem) = fidelity, love, strength, and protection

Sugar = sweetness and healing

Rose = love, luck, protection, healing, and love divination

Lavender = love, happiness, longevity, peace, protection, and purification

GREEN THUMB

The simplest way to attract love into your life is by planting a magnolia in your garden. The trees need slightly acidic, moist, loose, well-drained soil. To mimic their natural growing conditions, amend heavy soil with peat moss and compost. Magnolias grow best in areas where there is no winter freeze. They like full sun to partial shade and will benefit from regular watering in their first few years until established. Remember that they need lots of room to spread out!

DID YOU KNOW?

People have long used the bark of the magnolia tree, as it contains many natural compounds that are said to act as anti-inflammatory, anti-allergy, and antibacterial agents. The bark of the tree is an anxiolytic, which lowers anxiety and reduces stress. The world's oldest magnolia tree lives in Italy and is 320 years old!

∞ Magical ∞
Mindfulness Tip

Place a vase of magnolias next to your bed. Their magical scent will cheer you and whisk you gently off to the land of Nod.

(SWEET VIOLET)
(Viola)

Violets are diminutive plants whose flowers have five petals, most commonly in lavender and purple shades. The dark green leaves are usually heart-shaped and lobed. Because of purple's association with royalty, violets represent nobility, strength, and leadership. Ancient Greeks and Romans used violets to treat various ailments, as well as for making wine and sweetening dishes for their festivals.

2 GREEN WITCHES SAYETH

"To win a love who is dandy,
serve your beloved violet candy."

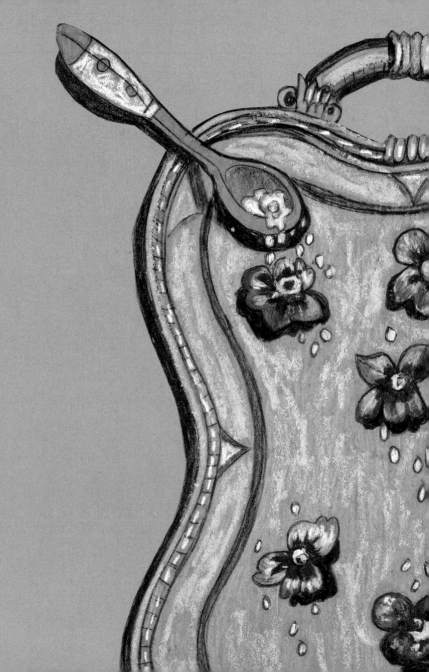

CANDIED VIOLET FLOWERS

(MAKES 30 CANDIED FLOWERS)

2 tablespoons aquafaba (the liquid from a can of chickpeas)
1 teaspoon water
30 violets, stems removed
Superfine sugar for sprinkling

Whisk aquafaba and water in a small bowl. Using a pair of tweezers to hold each flower, with a small basting brush gently brush on aquafaba mixture. Sprinkle with sugar. Place sugared flowers on a baking sheet covered with parchment paper. Do not stack flowers. Let stand at room temperature overnight.

These Candied Violet Flowers can last for several weeks if stored in a single layer in an airtight container at room temperature.

The following recipe is a bewitching way to incorporate candied violets into a wonderful dessert!

GLUTEN-FREE LEMON CUPCAKES WITH CANDIED VIOLETS

(MAKES 12 CUPCAKES)

CUPCAKES

1 ¾ cups gluten free all-purpose flour

1 cup organic sugar

1 teaspoon baking soda

½ teaspoon salt

1 cup cashew milk (any nut milk will do but we find cashew to be the richest)

⅓ cup organic extra virgin olive oil

1 teaspoon apple cider vinegar

1 teaspoon organic lemon extract

1 teaspoon vanilla extract

2 teaspoons organic lemon zest

36 Candied Violet Flowers (page 199), divided

LEMON FROSTING

3 cups powdered sugar

⅓ cup margarine

2 tablespoons organic lemon juice

1 teaspoon organic lemon zest

Preheat oven to 350°F.

Sift gluten-free flour with a mixer and add sugar, baking soda, and salt.

Then, add in cashew milk, extra virgin olive oil, apple cider vinegar, extracts, and lemon zest. Stir until combined. Divide the batter into cupcake trays with cupcake liners. Bake for 25 minutes.

Transfer baked cupcakes to a wire cooling rack and let cool completely before frosting.

In an electric mixing bowl, add in all lemon frosting ingredients. Mix, starting at slow speed, and gradually increase speed until frosting is smooth and thick.

Pipe frosting onto the cupcakes, then decorate with Candied Violet Flowers (3 per cupcake).

Enjoy with your love!

MAGICAL PROPERTIES OF GLUTEN-FREE LEMON CUPCAKES WITH CANDIED VIOLETS

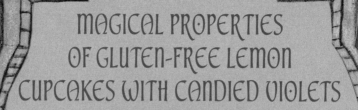

Violets = love, lust, protection, peace, and healing

Lemon = friendship, happiness, and love

Sugar = healing and sweetness

Olive (oil) = peace and friendship

Vanilla = love

Apple (cider vinegar) = love

Cashew (milk) = prosperity

GREEN THUMB

Violets are best grown from seed. They like full to partial sun. Violets can be directly seeded into your flower garden. Sow violet seeds early in the season and cover lightly with ⅛ inch of soil. Water every day until germination. (They germinate slowly.) You will notice their teeny tiny little leaves pop out of the soil. Violets prefer cool temperatures and wilt in midsummer's heat. In warmer areas, plant in partial shade. They tolerate a variety of soils. As you sow the seeds, say "May it be for love or lust, let violets grow in this dust."

❦ Magical ❧ Mindfulness Tip

Try growing a little flowerpot of magical violets in a sunny window. Keep soil moist to the touch but not soggy. These violets will bring peace and protection to your home.

DID YOU KNOW?

Napoleon Bonaparte declared the violet to be his signature flower. He covered his wife Josephine's grave in violets when she died in 1814. Violets are also very nutritious, containing high amounts of vitamin C. In fact, violets contain more vitamin C than many vegetables and fruits!

(Tree of Enchantment)

(Salix)

Willow trees are fast-growing deciduous plants known for their graceful drooping branches covered in bright green leaves. As a kid, I used our backyard willow as a fort, playing under its protective ground-length branches every day. The trees are captivating when they sway with the breeze. A willow tree can be cut back completely to the ground and will grow back several feet in the first year. Because of this tenacity, willows symbolize renewal and fertility.

2 GREEN WITCHES SAYETH

"Willow leaves carried in your pocket will bring you love fast as a rocket."

This is a simple spell and simple spells are our favorite kind! If you and your partner are hoping to get pregnant, simply place a willow branch under your bed to enhance the chances of conception. For that matter, if you're hoping to adopt, keeping a willow branch under the bed will help bring good luck with the adoption.

❧ Magical ❧
Mindfulness Tip

Find a nice big willow tree and take a long siesta underneath it. Bring a soft blanket, pillow, a lovely lunch, a bottle of your favorite beverage, and a good book. We love lounging with seed and gardening catalogs. A good grimoire is also recommended (hint, hint)!

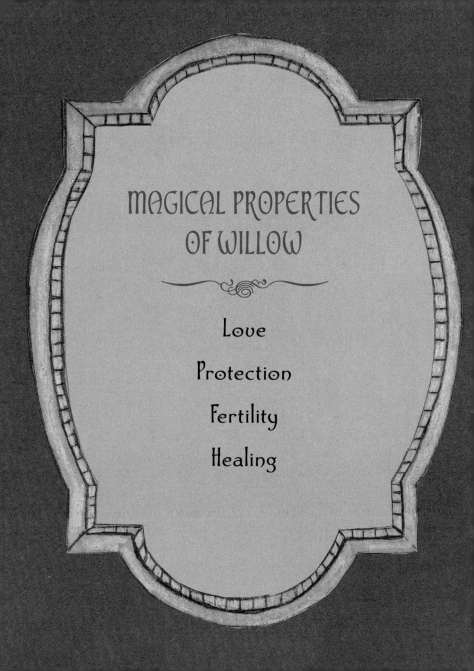

MAGICAL PROPERTIES
OF WILLOW

Love

Protection

Fertility

Healing

BRING MY LOVE TO ME AND SEAL THE DEAL SPELL

On a warm summer's day, write all the qualities you want in a partner with permanent marker on strips of red ribbon. Tie the ribbons together and wrap around the trunk of a willow tree while imagining your ideal partner. Should that person arrive while you are tying the ribbons, we suggest you two smooch right then and there under the privacy of the willow branches.

GREEN THUMB

You can grow a magical willow tree from cuttings. Take a cutting from a live terminal branch that is at least eighteen inches long. Insert the cut end into moist soil in a pot with good drainage or straight into garden soil. Keep it moderately moist until the cutting establishes roots. Another way is to grow from bare root trees that are at least a year old (ask at your local nursery). These need to have their roots soaked in a bucket before planting and soil worked to twice the depth and diameter of the root spread. Push soil in and around the roots when planting willow trees, and water the soil well. Consider carefully where you plant your tree or shrub. Not all types of willow trees are invasive, but many are and you do not want their root system all over your planting bed. Your new tree needs to be kept quite moist but not soggy as the roots establish. We recommend its first drink be a bucket of full moon water. Prune out old and dead wood. Willows flourish in moist organic-rich soils. If your soil is poor and has limited nutrients, work in compost at the time of planting and fertilize with an all-purpose plant food in early spring. Water willows in periods of drought. *Warning*: Never plant near plumbing or irrigation pipes. Your willow will tear them up in search of water. She is such a thirsty tree!

DID YOU KNOW?

The tradition of knocking on wood for good luck came from the ancient Celts. They believed that if you knock on a willow tree, it will send away bad luck. To this day, many use the expression "knock on wood" to add luck to a situation.

XYLOBIUM ORCHID

(Orchidaceae)

Orchids are renowned for their elegant, shimmering, waxy flowers of many colors. Orchids are epiphytes from the tropics.They live in trees as "guest" plants in tropical areas of the world. Plants bloom once yearly and have two to three large green leaves. Flowers blossom at the end of a long, fairly sturdy stem. They bloom once a year and make showy indoor plants.

2 GREEN WITCHES SAYETH

"Wear a chain of orchid flowers in your hair and Venus will bring you a love pure and fair."

MAGICAL FLOWER CROWN
TO ATTRACT LOVE

1 (24-gauge) wire
Xylobium or any kind of orchid flowers
Assorted smaller flowers such as yarrow and baby's breath
Floral tape stem wrap or twine
1 tube floral adhesive

Connect two pieces of wire by twisting the ends to a size that will easily fit the crown of your head.

Trim your flowers so that you have about 3 to 4 inches of stem

Wire each flower stem to give them added support so that they don't droop.

Wrap the entire stem around the wire with floral tape or twine.

Attach flowers to the wire crown by twisting their stems around and securing them with floral tape. Fill in using the same method with smaller flowers around the larger orchids as you go, adding floral adhesive to secure them.

If you're not going to wear your crown right away, store it in the refrigerator.

MAGICAL PROPERTIES OF XYLOBIUM ORCHIDS

Love

Lust

Potency

GREEN THUMB

Most orchids prefer to be grown in a loose potting mix of soil and bark. Nurseries sell specific growing mix just for orchids. Drench the potting mix with water until it runs out of the bottom of the pot. Let the growing mix dry out before watering again. Orchids like to have their leaves misted occasionally to imitate the moist climates where they originate. Place your orchid in indirect light, a north or east facing window is ideal. Cut back bloom stems that have died. Your magical orchids should bloom once a year.

❧ Magical ❧ Mindfulness Tip

Know anyone who works in an office? Many offices buy orchids to cheer up the work environment, then sadly toss the orchids in the garbage when they stop blooming. Boo. We green witches know that orchids are perennials that rebloom every year. It will do your heart a world of good to do what we do. Adopt them and keep them watered and misted, in a partly sunny window, until they burst open with another round of blooms!

DID YOU KNOW?

When dinosaurs roamed the earth approximately 120 million years ago, the planet was covered in primordial forests, and flowering plants were just starting to emerge. Among the very first of those flowering plants was the orchid. By the mid-nineteenth century, a younger species on earth called humans were experiencing an orchid mania. So fashionable were orchids that Queen Victoria even had a royal orchid grower.

(Seven Years Love)

(Achillea millefolium)

Yarrow is a member of the aster family with flat-topped clusters of tiny delicate flowers in a range of hues including white, yellow, red, pink, and gold. Yarrow is perennial and can reach a height of three feet. They are beloved by butterflies who use their flat mass of flowers as landing pads. The pale green leaves are hairy and ferny in appearance. Yarrow is a cottage garden favorite that every green witch should grow.

2 GREEN WITCHES SAYETH

"Dried yarrow over your bed shall release your fears, and your marriage will be happy for at least seven years."

YARROW LOVE TEA

(SERVES 2)

- 2 cups water
- 2 teaspoons dried yarrow flowers
- 1–2 teaspoons maple syrup or organic sugar, to taste (optional)

In a medium saucepan, combine water and yarrow flowers and bring to a boil.

Remove from heat and let steep for 10 minutes to reach potency. Strain through a fine mesh sieve into a teapot or container. Be sure to compost discarded solids!

Mix in maple syrup or sugar for a sweeter tea.

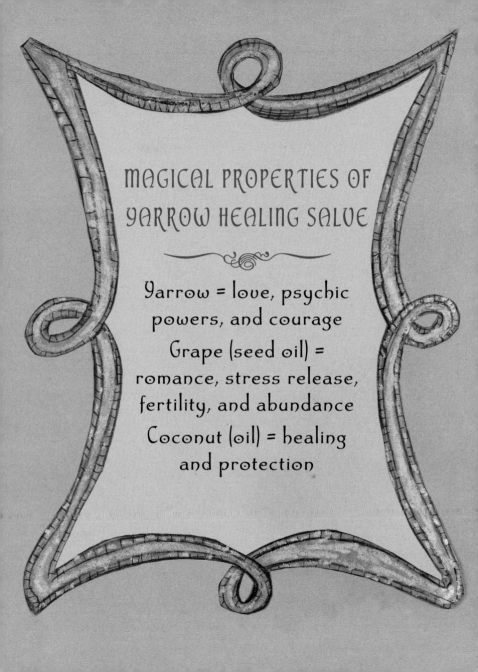

MAGICAL PROPERTIES OF YARROW HEALING SALVE

Yarrow = love, psychic powers, and courage

Grape (seed oil) = romance, stress release, fertility, and abundance

Coconut (oil) = healing and protection

YARROW
HEALING SALVE

This moisturizing salve is great for rubbing on rashes and flaky dry skin.

½ cup dried yarrow, flowers and leaves
1 cup grape seed oil
1 ounce coconut oil

In a small jar, add yarrow and cover with grapeseed oil. Let infuse for 2 days. Strain.

Transfer yarrow oil to the top pan of a double boiler kept over low heat. Add the coconut oil and heat until oil has just melted. Stir to combine.

Transfer to a sterilized jar with a lid and leave to cool.

Store in a cool, dry place for up to 1 month.

ᚚ Magical ᚚ
Mindfulness Tip

As a little gift to yourself, make a cup of yarrow tea using the flowers and leaves (fresh or dried). Let it cool and use as an astringent on your face to freshen and tighten pores.

GREEN THUMB

Plant around the time of the Flower Moon in May. Provide full sun and consistent water in its first year of growing, then let it adapt to less water in year two. Yarrow is evergreen in warm climates. Cut back dead foliage in winter.

DID YOU KNOW?

Throughout history, yarrow has been well known as an anti-inflammatory and an antimicrobial. It is reported to reduce pain, relax circulation, and is considered a mild sedative. Burning dried yarrow as incense will fight off negativity. Yarrow has been used for ages to treat fevers. Yarrow (*Achillea millefolium*) was named after the Greek mythical hero Achilles, who used the herb to stop the bleeding wounds of his soldiers during the Trojan War in 1200 BCE.

(Zinnia violacea)

Zinnias are annuals with daisy-like flower heads on sturdy stems in all colors of the rainbow, even green. Sometimes the petals come in many layers and form a saucer shape. Zinnias have long been considered a flower of platonic love, like the love you might have with an old friend. We say "old" friend because zinnias are symbolic of long-lasting relationships. It's the kind of friendship where even if you haven't seen each other in ages, you pick right up where you left off. Zinnias bloom from spring until autumn. They make great cut flowers.

2 GREEN WITCHES SAYETH

"A pot of zinnias will bring love to you,
And love to the birds, bees, and butterflies too!"

BEST FRIENDS FOREVER (BFF) GIFT

This is a great gift to give a friend who you haven't seen in a long time.

1 (10-inch) clay pot and water tray
1 small can pink outdoor paint
1 medium bag organic top soil
1 packet pink zinnia seeds
1 packet red zinnia seeds
2 popsicle sticks
1 stapler
1 red ribbon

Paint the outside of a clay pot using your favorite shade of pink. Fill the pot with top soil to about 2 inches from the top and lightly tamp down the soil. Open the seed packets carefully, tearing just along the very bottom edge. Mix the seeds up and gently push them into the soil until the soil reaches the top of your fingernail. Slide a popsicle stick into the bottom of each seed packet, then staple the packet to secure it. You will have made two pretty little signs that show your friend what they can expect when the seeds grow. Tie a red ribbon around the pot and gift it to your BFF. They will think fondly of you as their zinnias grow and bloom.

ᘓ Magical ᘔ Mindfulness Tip

Plant zinnias in the garden or windowsill in remembrance of a loved one. This could also be for a pet who has crossed the rainbow bridge. They are a lovely memorial when planted at a grave site. If you are considering getting a tattoo in honor of a lost loved one, you might consider adding zinnias to the design as a symbol that they will never be forgotten.

MAGICAL PROPERTIES
OF ZINNIAS

Thoughts of faraway friends
Long-lasting love
Remembrance
Affection

GREEN THUMB

Magical zinnias are a cinch to grow. Plant zinnia seeds in spring in rich, compost-y soil. Zinnias like full sun and regular water and will bloom into autumn. Zinnias are a huge draw for bees, butterflies, and hummingbirds. Enjoy the show!

DID YOU KNOW?

Butterflies are especially drawn to zinnias and find their bright colors and nectar irresistible. If you're planting a butterfly garden (and everyone should), you will want to plant many zinnias along with butterfly host plants such as milkweed and dill. Zinnias are native to Mexico and have been grown in gardens since the time of the Aztecs. Zinnias are named after eighteenth-century German botanist Johann G. Zinn.

THE POWER OF LOVE
DINNER FOR TWO

(ALL RECIPES SERVE 2 WITH LEFTOVERS)

Certain foods have been known to be aphrodisiacs, some for their love magic, and some for their resemblance to male and female body parts. Make this special vegan aphrodisiac dinner when you want to invoke the mother of all love spells! *Candlelight required.*

Menu

POMEGRANATE CHAMPAGNE PUNCH

Since ancient times, pomegranates have been considered an aphrodisiac. According to Greek mythology, Hades, king of the underworld, did not want to lose Persephone, his beloved, so he gave her pomegranate seeds to win her heart.

½ cup water
½ cup organic sugar
1 (750-milliliter) bottle chilled Brut Champagne or prosecco
¼ cup white rum
¼ cup organic pomegranate juice
1 organic orange, thinly sliced
Pomegranate seeds
Fresh mint leaves

Bring water and sugar to boil in a small saucepan, stirring until sugar dissolves. Simmer 5 minutes. Cool syrup completely. Then, fill a glass pitcher with ice and add in Champagne or prosecco, rum, and pomegranate juice. Add enough of the simple syrup to taste (you will not need all the syrup). Stir gently to combine. Pour into Champagne or wine glasses and garnish with orange slices, pomegranate seeds, and mint leaves.

∼ LOVE POWER ∼

Rum is made from molasses, honey, or sugarcane, which makes for a very sweet romance. Oranges are known for love magic and fertility. Champagne is definitely the most romantic of all libations. Throughout history, alcohol has served as the basis for most love philtres.

WALNUT AND VEGAN BLUE CHEESE-STUFFED FIGS

5 fresh Black Mission or Turkish figs
Balsamic vinegar
Salt and pepper, to taste
4 ounces vegan blue cheese (White Rabbit Kitchen or Vremery Brand recommended)
½ cup walnuts, quartered and toasted

Preheat the oven to 350°F. Slice the figs in half lengthwise and place on a baking pan. Create a small opening in the middle of each fig with a teaspoon or a melon baller. Drizzle the fig halves with 2 or 3 drops of balsamic vinegar and sprinkle with salt and pepper. Fill each fig with a little cheese and top with a quarter of a walnut. Bake for 5 minutes and serve warm.

⬯ LOVE POWER ⬯

Figs contain flavonoids, polyphenols, and antioxidants, which can strengthen sexual endurance. Walnuts contain essential fatty acids and vitamins A, E, B1, and B2 and provide a great energy boost.

TAGLIATELLE WITH WILD MUSHROOMS AND TRUFFLE OIL

⅔ ounces dried morel or porcini mushrooms
1 cup boiling-hot water
2 tablespoons organic extra virgin olive oil, divided
¾ pound mixed fresh wild mushrooms (such as cremini, oyster,
   chanterelle, or porcini), washed, trimmed, and sliced lengthwise
3 medium garlic cloves, minced
Salt and pepper, to taste
½ pound dried tagliatelle pasta, fresh or dried
2 tablespoons fresh flat-leaf parsley, chopped
1 teaspoon organic lemon zest, finely grated
½ teaspoon organic lemon juice
2 teaspoons truffle oil
2 tablespoons vegan parmesan cheese, grated

Soak dried mushrooms in boiling-hot water in a bowl until softened,
about 20 minutes. Drain and pat dry. Finely chop mushrooms and
set aside. Heat 1 tablespoon olive oil in a heavy skillet over medium
heat and sauté fresh mushrooms with garlic, salt, and pepper, stirring
occasionally until mushrooms are browned, about 5 to 7 minutes. Stir in
soaked mushrooms and simmer 1 minute, then remove from heat.

Bring a large pot of water to boil. Add pasta and cook until al dente according to package instructions. Drain. Add pasta to mushroom mixture in skillet along with remaining oil and cook over medium heat for a few additional minutes. Remove from heat.

Add parsley, lemon zest, lemon juice, and truffle oil and toss well. Garnish with vegan parmesan cheese and fresh cracked pepper, to taste.

❧ LOVE POWER ❧

Mushrooms contain high amounts of protein and zinc, which are said to increase sexual energy. Truffles and morels are considered to be the most potent of all fungi.

ROASTED ASPARAGUS WITH TOMATOES AND PINE NUTS

1 pound fresh organic asparagus, trimmed
½ cup organic grape tomatoes, halved
3 tablespoons pine nuts
2 tablespoons organic extra virgin olive oil
2 garlic cloves, minced
Salt and pepper, to taste
1 tablespoon organic lemon juice
1 teaspoon organic lemon zest

Preheat oven to 400°F. Place the asparagus, tomatoes, and pine nuts on a foil-lined baking pan. In a separate bowl, mix together oil, garlic, salt, and pepper; add to asparagus and toss to coat. Bake 15 to 20 minutes or just until asparagus is tender. Drizzle with lemon juice; sprinkle with pepper and lemon zest. Toss to combine.

❧ LOVE POWER ☙

Asparagus has high amounts of vitamins A, B, and C and is believed to have a stimulating effect on sexual desire. Ancient Romans referred to pine nuts as "love kernels." They contain a high amount of protein and fat and are considered a particularly strong aphrodisiac. Tomatoes can ignite passion and were once known as "love apples" in sixteenth-century France and Italy.

COCONUT AND CHOCOLATE MOUSSE WITH STRAWBERRY COULIS

COCONUT AND CHOCOLATE MOUSSE

1 can coconut milk or coconut cream (do not use low-fat)
¼ cup Dutch-process cocoa or any extra rich cocoa powder
3 tablespoons confectioners' sugar
½ teaspoon pure vanilla extract
½ teaspoon instant espresso powder
1 teaspoon brandy or cognac
Fresh strawberries and mint leaves, to garnish

STRAWBERRY COULIS

1 cup frozen unsweetened organic strawberries
½ cup organic sugar
1 tablespoon organic lemon juice

TO SERVE

Fresh strawberries
Mint leaves

Continued on next page

Refrigerate the coconut milk or cream overnight (or freeze for about 10 to 20 minutes). Once chilled, open the milk or cream and transfer only the thick coconut cream to a bowl (the cream and water should have separated). Discard the coconut water or save for another recipe. Using a handheld electric mixer, whip the cream until smooth and thick. Add remaining mousse ingredients and whip until it forms a creamy mousse-like texture. Divide into small teacups or ramekins and chill for at least one hour or overnight.

In a medium saucepan, combine the strawberry coulis ingredients. Bring to a boil over medium-high heat. Let cool. Transfer to a food processor and puree until smooth. Strain with a fine mesh strainer and set aside. Store coulis in a sealed glass jar in the refrigerator for up to 1 week.

To serve, garnish each cup with 1 tablespoon of strawberry coulis, fresh strawberries, and mint leaves.

⊙℞ LOVE POWER ℗⊙

The Aztecs and Mayans were the first to recognize the potency of chocolate. The Aztec ruler Montezuma was said to drink fifty cups of chocolate per day to better serve his harem of six hundred! Vanilla is a powerful sexual plant that creates a feeling of comfort and peace. Coconut holds the power of the Great Mother Moon and can help us to be more loving and understanding. Strawberries contain zinc and sharpen the senses.

ADDITIONAL PLANTS FOR CREATING LOVE MAGIC

Note: We suggest buying and growing organic whenever possible!

Cayenne pepper (*Capsicum annuum*)
Recommended use: Literally spice up a meal using a powdered form!

Cinnamon (*Cinnamomum cassia*)
Recommended use: As a spice in sweet or savory dishes. You can also boil cinnamon sticks for a soothing tea.

Coriander (*Coriandrum sativum*)
Recommended use: Sachets.

Hemp (*Cannibus sativa*)
Recommended use: CBD oils can be ingested or added to baths or lotions.

Henbane (*Hyosycamus niger*)
Recommended use: Pin it to your outer garment. *Warning*: Henbane is poisonous to ingest.

Hibiscus (*Hibiscus rosa-sinensis*)
Recommended use: The flowers and leaves may be boiled to make a lovely tea for two.

Lemongrass (*Cymbopogon citratus*)
Recommended use: The tender inner stalks of the plant are delicious in salads, stir-fries, or sauces.

Lettuce (*Lactuca Sativa*)
Recommended use: Toss into a healthy salad for two.

Marjoram (*Origanum majorana*)
Recommended use: Add it as a spice to your cooking.

Sugar cane (*Saccharum officinarum*)
Recommended use: Make sweet treats for your beloved.

Tomato (*Lycopersicon spp.*)
Recommended use: Eat on its own or cooked in a recipe.

Vanilla (*Vanilla aromitica*)
Recommended use: As a spice in cooking for something sweet.

Yerba mate: (*Ilex paraguariensis*)
Recommended use: Make a tea to share with your loved one.

☙ How to Break a Love Spell ❧

(Just in case!)

Eating pistachios (*Pistachia vera*) will negate any love spell—by either party. If you are allergic to nuts, a tea made with wild geranium flowers (*Geranium maculatum*) can also be used to erase a love spell.

❧ GLOSSARY ❧

ACHILLES: In Greek mythology, he was the hero of the Trojan War and the fiercest of all Greek warriors.

ADONIS: A beautiful youth from Greek mythology. He was the mortal lover of Aphrodite, goddess of love and beauty, and of Persephone, goddess of the underworld.

ALTAR: From the Latin word for "high," this term refers to a raised sacred space that people use during times of reflection.

ANNUAL: A plant that grows only for one season within a year.

APHRODISIAC: A food or drink that stimulates sexual desire.

APHRODITE: The ancient Greek goddess associated with love, beauty, pleasure, and passion. Aphrodite's major symbols include apples, roses, and swans.

APOLLO: The ancient Greek god of the sun, music, and prophecy. He was also considered to be one of the most handsome and virile of all gods.

AQUAFABA: The common name for the liquid in a can of chickpeas. Aquafaba can be used to replace egg whites in many sweet and savory recipes.

ARCHEMORUS: In Greek mythology, he was the son of Lycurgus of Nemea. Archemorus literally means "the forerunner of death" and as an infant he was killed by a serpent.

BALM: A fragrant ointment or preparation used to heal or soothe the skin.

BANISH: Driving away any unwanted energy, habit, person, or thing that is undesirable or unhealthy for you.

CANDLE MAGIC: A type of ritual that calls on the element of fire to bring greater energy and power into the physical world.

CAULDRON: A large metal pot with a lid and handle that is used for cooking over an open fire. Tiny ones are typically used for burning incense.

CBD OIL: Derived from the cannabis plant and reported to possess health benefits that include reducing pain and inflammation. CBD oil is non-hallucinogenic.

CHARM: A magical means of influencing the outcome of a situation by use of a crafted object that a witch imbues with a specific energy.

CLEANSING: To rid any sort of negative energy affecting you. A candle cleansing or sage burning are two rituals that can be used to cleanse your surroundings.

CONJURING: To summon a spirit by magical or supernatural power.

COTTAGE GARDEN: An informally designed garden with a mixture of ornamental and edible plants. English in origin.

COVEN: A group or gathering of witches who meet regularly.

CRYSTALS: A holistic, noninvasive, energy-based system of healing in which crystals are placed either on or around the body. Witches often carry crystals in their pockets to take their power with them.

CUPID: The ancient Roman god of love and the son of Mars and Venus. Cupid (Eros in Greek mythology) is represented as a winged, naked, infant boy with a bow and arrows.

DAISY CHAIN: A series of interwoven daisies used to make a garland.

DEADHEAD: The act of removing dead flower heads from a plant to encourage additional blooming.

DIVINATION: The seeking of information by supernatural means such as tarot cards, pendulums, crystals, and plants.

ECHO: The mountain nymph from Ovid's *Metamorphoses*. She tempted the beautiful youth Narcissus who rejected her and fell in love with his own reflection.

ELIXIR: A magical or medicinal potion.

ELVEN: Considered lively, often mischievous entity. Elven is the term for elf in Middle English.

EROS: In Greek mythology, Eros is the god of love and the son of Aphrodite. Eros is a Greek word which means desire.

FAIRY: A mythical being of folklore and romance usually having diminutive human form and possessing magic powers. Fairies are guardians of plants. They are sometimes called devas.

FAMILIAR: A household pet that serves as a witch's companion and loyal protector. The cat has long been the most popular animal to become a familiar.

FLOWER MOON: The full moon in May when the spring flowers are in bloom. Also known as the planting moon.

GARDEN WITCH: Another name for a green witch. They are also known as hedge witches, forest witches, or kitchen witches.

THE GREAT PLAGUE: An outbreak of bubonic plague in England in 1665–1666 in which about one fifth of the population of London died.

THE GREAT SPIRIT: The representation of God in many Native American traditions, particularly Algonquian and Siouan tribes.

GREEK MYTHOLOGY: Stories originally told by the ancient Greeks concerning the origin and nature of the world and the lives of deities, heroes, and mythological creatures.

GREEN WITCHCRAFT: A magical practice that focuses on the materials and energies of the natural world.

GRIMOIRE: A book that contains any kind of magical information. A witch's personal grimoire is as unique as the witch who made it.

HADES: In Greek mythology, Hades is the god of the underworld and the underground home of the dead.

HEDGE WITCH: Another name for a green witch. The term is an homage to the wise old women who often lived on the outskirts of villages, beyond the hedge.

HEMIPARASITE: A plant which gains nutrients by feeding off of another plant.

HERB: Any plant with leaves, seeds, and flowers used for flavoring, food, medicine, or perfume.

HYACINTH: In Greek mythology, Hyacinth was a very beautiful Spartan prince and lover of the god Apollo.

INCANTATION: A series of words said as a magic spell or charm.

INVOKE: To call forth by incantation.

KAMA: In Hindu traditions, Kama is the god of erotic desire.

KITCHEN WITCH: A witch who focuses their magical practice on the home and hearth and uses things commonly found in the kitchen as magical tools.

MABON: One of the eight Wiccan sabbats celebrated during the second harvest and equinox. It is a time for giving thanks.

MONTEZUMA: The last fully independent ruler of the Aztec empire before the civilization's collapse at the hands of the Spanish in the early sixteenth century.

MOON MOTHER: A woman who helps other women awaken their authentic and creative self.

MOON WATER: Water that has sat out all night being energized under a full moon.

MOTHER EARTH: Used to refer to the planet earth as a woman or a goddess.

NARCISSUS: In Greek mythology, Narcissus is a beautiful youth who rejected the nymph Echo and fell in love with his own reflection in a pool.

NEMESIS: The Greek goddess of revenge. She was considered to be a remorseless goddess.

PAGAN: A person with religious beliefs other than those of the main world religions. Pagans often worship earth or nature.

PERENNIAL: A plant that comes back year after year.

PHEROMONE: A chemical substance produced by an animal that affects the behavior of another of its species.

PHILTRE: A love potion.

POMANDER: A piece of fruit (often an orange or apple) studded with aromatic herbs such as cloves, lavender, and rosemary. Often used as air fresheners.

POTION: A liquid with healing, magical, or poisonous properties.

RITUAL: A sequence of activities using gestures, words, actions, or objects.

ROSE QUARTZ: A translucent pink variety of quartz. The most popular and powerful uses for rose quartz are for attracting love and partnership.

SACHET: A small cloth bag filled with herbs, stones, and/or aromatic ingredients.

SACRED SPACE: Any dedicated area that has been set aside for worship, prayer, meditation, or rituals.

SALICYLIC ACID: A bitter compound present in certain plants. It is used as a fungicide and in the manufacturing of aspirin and dyestuffs.

SPELL: A magical ritual to move energy and create manifestation. A spell can involve the use of spoken words as well as objects such as herbs, candles, and oils.

TINCTURE: A concentrated herbal extract made by soaking bark, berries, leaves, or roots in alcohol or vinegar.

TROJAN WAR: In Greek mythology, the Trojan War was waged against the city of Troy. It was caused by Paris, son of the Trojan king, and Helen, wife of Greek king Menelaus, when they went off together to Troy. To get her to return, Menelaus sought help from his brother Agamemnon, who assembled a Greek army to defeat Troy.

VENUS: The planet of beauty and love is the brightest planet visible to the human eye. It is the second nearest planet to the sun after mercury. Venus is also the Roman goddess of love.

WARD: To ward is to invoke a magical boundary of protection around a property or sacred space.

WITCH: A person credited with supernatural powers.

ZEPHYR: The Greek god of the west wind which was considered the gentlest of the winds.

ᴄᴋ RECOMMENDED READING ᴐᴅ

The Secret Teachings of Plants by Stephen Harrod Buhner
The Lost Language of Plants by Stephen Harrod Buhner
Cunningham's Encyclopedia of Magical Herbs by Scott Cunningham
The Legend of the Indian Paintbrush by Tomie DePaola
Garden Witchery by Ellen Dugan
Wildflowers on the Windowsill by Susan Tyler Hitchcock
Speaking with Nature by Sandra Ingerman & Llyn Roberts
Circe by Madeline Miller
Green Witchcraft by Ann Moura
The House Witch by Arin Murphy-Hiscock
Green Witch by Arin Murphy-Hiscock
The Illustrated Herbiary by Maia Toll
Healing Wise by Susun S. Weed
Nature's Remedies by Jean Willoughby & Katie Shelly

✺ ACKNOWLEDGMENTS ✺

This book would not have been possible without the support of the following people.

A special shout-out to Nicole Mele, our editor at Skyhorse, and to our agent, Lisa Hagan, for believing in this book. Thanks to Jade Lee for her original design concept and to Tucker Shaw and Jon Kinnally for editing and reading early drafts.

We would also like to thank Christy Ottaviano, Ted Ottaviano, Paul Zakris, Dave Skwarczek, Steven Kolb, Jessi Klein, Tonya Hurley, Dan Mathews, Veronica Varlow, kac young, Mario Pulice, Noah Fecks, Justin Belmondo, Ethan Lunkenheimer, Sarah Hall, Billy Norwich, Tracy Poust, Monica Kaye, Carolyn Joyce, Nora Burns, Liadan Leonard, Debbie Harry, and Jing and Chris at Alta Images.

CHRIS WOULD LIKE TO THANK

I dedicate this book to the bewitching Jon Kinnally.

Big thanks to:

Irma, Jessi Klein, Laura Basset, Jade Lee, Tracy Poust, Monica Kaye, Gina Chai, Sarah Hall, Dave Skwarczek, Kelly Kiseskey, Lisa Bagley, Lisa Hagan, Nicole Mele, Bridget Wolfe, John Curtis Crawford, Loretta Hively, Stacey Thamba, Lesley Brown, and Debbie Harry. Gratitude to my familiars: Ching, Kyeoshi, Maggie, Chaos, Kitty, Maria, Fred, Simon, Elliott, and Howard.

Finally, big love to my favorite green witch, Susan, for going on this journey with me!

SUSAN WOULD LIKE TO THANK

Ted Ottaviano, my forever collaborator who continues to inspire and focus every project I attempt. Tucker Shaw for a lifetime of support, understanding, and Saturday morning phone calls. Paul Zakris, for being a great husband and my talented art director. Jade Lee, for forty years of friendship and creativity. Love to Lisa Hagan (I am so glad that you are part of my life again) and to Christy Ottaviano, sister and editrix extraordinaire.

A special thanks to Chris for his talent and patience to grow our little idea into a beautiful flower!

Meow to Circe, my black kitty.

ABOUT THE AUTHORS

Follow Susan and Chris on Instagram @2greenwitches

CHRIS YOUNG

Chris believes all plants are magical. He is a lifelong gardener whose acclaimed garden, **Tiny Sur,** is a certified wildlife habitat, which boasts thousands of online followers. He was lucky enough to meet a green witch when he was young who taught him about the magical properties and uses of many plants. These teachings along with his own research have led this former **Comedy Central** executive to create this book.

His garden writing has been featured in such publications as **WestCoast Magazine, Country Living,** and **L.A. Parent Magazine.** Chris's interactive children's book *Is That a Fairy?* was published by Storypanda.

SUSAN OTTAVIANO

Artist, performer, and songwriter Susan Ottaviano's career has taken her from the recording studio as the lead singer for the band **Book of Love** to the photo studio as a food stylist for clients like **Bon Appétit** and **Grey Goose**. Along with her partner in **2 Green Witches**, Chris Young, she's thrilled to share her magical world of flora and fauna in this book.